IMAGES
of America

LEON VALLEY

This aerial view of downtown Leon Valley from the 1940s shows only farmland with a few homes along the roads. A hangar and planes of an airport used during World War II on Grissom Road can be seen at the lower left. The hangar is still in use today as a storage building. It is owned by Uhl's Storage and the name has recently been changed to Leon Valley Storage. (Courtesy of Kenneth and Esther Alley Historical Collection.)

ON THE COVER: Members of this bowling party on the back patio of Skinny's Café had their photograph taken on August 6, 1947. Their names are all listed on the back but are too numerous to be listed here. Many are descendents of the early settlers of Leon Valley. The café was later named the Texas Star Inn and is currently doing business as Grady's Barbecue. The original image was taken by Joe Bacon in his collection of photographs of San Antonio, Texas. (Courtesy of Gloria Anderson.)

IMAGES
of America

LEON VALLEY

Friends of the Leon Valley Public Library
and Leon Valley Historical Society

ARCADIA
PUBLISHING

Published by Arcadia Publishing
Charleston, South Carolina

Library of Congress Control Number: 2011932825

For all general information, please contact Arcadia Publishing:
Telephone 843-853-2070
Fax 843-853-0044
E-mail sales@arcadiapublishing.com
For customer service and orders:
Toll-Free 1-888-313-2665

Visit us on the Internet at www.arcadiapublishing.com

*This book is dedicated to all those who have steadfastly
worked to preserve and keep Leon Valley's history alive.*

CONTENTS

ACKNOWLEDGMENTS

This book came into being because of a need to continue chronicling the history of the Leon Valley area and its people. The Kenneth and Esther Alley Historical Collection (K&EAHC) was an excellent source of information. The *Leon Valley Sesquicentennial Cookbook* published in 1985 and the revised edition published in 2002 contained many family histories contributed by longtime residents of Leon Valley, including Karen Peterson, Gloria Anderson, Charlotte Asch, Kenneth Alley, Barbara Fryer, Linda Persyn, and Joyce Trent. The research team of the Leon Valley Historical Society (LVHS)—Linda Persyn, Kenneth Alley, Barbara Fryer, and Catherine Meaney—documented much of the early history of the Huebner and Onion families.

Many others contributed their knowledge and expertise to the compilation of this book. Gloria Anderson, early member of the Leon Valley Pageant Association, shared her memory album. Kenneth and Virginia Evers shared their family stories and photographs. Sharon Cunningham greatly assisted in the early revision and editing. Bea Miller helped with the fine tuning of the manuscript. Peggy Bissett and Peggy Proffitt assisted with the captions as did Joyce Trent. Carol Poss wrote most of the captions and compiled the manuscript along with scanning the photographs. We are grateful for the editing and computer assistance of Beth Poss Baker and the photographic expertise and computer talents of Sherry Watson. Special thanks to all those individuals who contributed photographs and information, and they are the following: Gloria Anderson, Geri Scarborough, Shirley Owen, Dorothy Wright, Horace Staph, J. Lee Neely III, Grace Nixon, Barbara Fryer, Jill Hand, Sherry Watson, and Donna Maytum Christopher. The Leon Valley Public Library (LVPL), the Northside Independent School District website, the W.Z. Burke Elementary School, and the P.I. Nixon Medical Historical Library also supplied photographs and/or information.

The Arcadia book on *Helotes* written by Cynthia Leal Massey proved to be an invaluable guide and pattern to follow in the compilation of our book. Finally, we would like to thank our editor, Lauren Hummer, for her assistance and working patiently with us in this exciting venture.

INTRODUCTION

The city of Leon Valley is located 10 miles northwest of San Antonio on Texas State Highway 16. Leon Creek, named by Spanish explorers in the 1700s, flows near the city. Leon is the Spanish name for lion. It is said that mountain lions once roamed the area along the creek. In 1924, when the first public school was established in the area, school board member Henry Steubing suggested that the school be named Leon Valley. Before that time, the area was considered to be a part of Helotes, Texas.

Even in ancient times, Native American tribes often camped along the streams of the Leon Valley area. Long before the Spaniards and Europeans arrived, the Native Americans had an ancient history and lived according to their own laws and oral traditions. In the 1940s, a Native American burial site was discovered on the west bank of Leon Creek near Bandera Road. A young woman was found buried in a sitting position, facing west with yellow paint on her face and hair. The manner of burial suggests she was of the Tonkawa tribe. After determining the age of the Indian woman, her remains were taken to the Witte Museum in San Antonio. More than 1,000 arrow points have been found in Leon Valley, as well as the tusk of a Mastodon.

In the 1800s, many Europeans immigrated to Texas, and some of them settled in the Leon Valley area. Among them were the Bormann, Steubing, Evers, and Huebner families. They established thriving ranches and dairy farms.

Fredrick "Fritz" Bormann (1835–1916) immigrated from Pommern, Prussia, in 1856. During the Civil War, he served in the Union army. He was wounded twice and walked with a limp. His farm was located on Poss Road near Raymond Rimkus Park. In 1869, he married Katherine Schoen (1845–1919) of New Braunfels. Bormann cut hay from the prairie and sold it to the army. On one of these hay-hauling trips, Indians scalped his business partner.

Heinrich Steubing Sr. (1832–1915) was born in Bicken, Germany, and came to New Braunfels when he was 16 years old. During the Civil War, he was conscripted into the Confederate army. He was captured and sent to a prison in New York. He and a friend escaped, and he walked back to his home in Texas. He married Katherine Wetz (1841–1872). Katherine died in 1872 after the birth of her last child. Heinrich remarried, and his family moved in 1885 to Leon Creek, where he and his sons owned several farms. Steubing's farm was at the corner of Texas Highway 16 and Eckhert Road on the Leon Creek.

Claus Evers (1818–1900) and his wife, Johanna Bochen Evers (1818–1905), emigrated from Schleswig-Holstein, Germany, in 1855 with their son Christian (1847–1915) and daughter Christina (1850–?). Their son Christian Evers owned a large dairy farm on Evers Road in Leon Valley and donated land for the first school in Leon Valley. He married Christine Buck, and they had 10 children. Christina Evers, the daughter of Claus and Johanna, married Frank Wehmeyer. Three days after the birth of their third child, Frank Wehmeyer died. Christina married Christian Braendle, and they had seven children.

Joseph Huebner (1823–1882) with his wife, Caroline (?–1923), and their two children, Anna (age seven) and Franz (age five), emigrated from Gablonz, Austria, in 1853. He purchased 184 acres of land that was 10 miles northwest of San Antonio in August 1858 and built his homestead in 1862. Over the next 20 years, he purchased 800 acres and built his herds of cattle, mules, and horses. He established a stagecoach stop where passengers could rest and horses could be exchanged. Joseph Huebner is buried on the land adjacent to the homestead. In April 1930, Judge John Onion and his family moved into the homestead.

Many other pioneers contributed to the early settlement of the Leon Valley area. Among them were the Eckart, Reininger, Hein, Kneupper, Ehler, Salazar, Nixon, Poss, and Guilbeau families.

The local families established a private school in 1894, called Evers School, at the corner of Evers Road and Huebner Road. In 1924, the first public school, Leon Valley School, was established. It is located at the corner of Texas State Highway 16 and Grissom Road and is presently the Northside Independent School District Museum and Learning Center. That same year, the Evers School was moved to the new location. It served as a teachers' home from 1924 through the 1950s, when it was demolished to provide space for the construction of new classrooms and an office.

During the 1920s, Joseph Dietsch and Anna Siedo Dietsch owned a general store on Texas State Highway 16 across the street from the Leon Valley School. In the late 1930s, Raymond Rimkus opened a general store and butcher shop at the corner of Texas Highway 16 near Leon Valley School. Rimkus became the first mayor of the City of Leon Valley. In 1952, it was rumored that the City of San Antonio was about to annex with the Leon Valley area. Local citizens quickly united and applied to the State of Texas to incorporate. The City of Leon Valley incorporation was approved on March 29, 1952.

Leon Valley gradually evolved from a ranching and farming community to a thriving city whose civic leaders saw a need to celebrate and preserve its history. They established the Leon Valley Pageant Association in 1973, which commemorated its early history with a Stagecoach Days Parade and other events. One of the organizations within the Leon Valley Pageant Association was the Leon Valley Historical Society. The purpose of this group was to research, document, and celebrate the history of Leon Valley and its surrounding area. Today, the Leon Valley Historical Society maintains the historical archives located in the Leon Valley Public Library, sponsors history-related events and activities, and is fundraising to restore the Huebner-Onion Stagecoach Stop.

In May 1977, a grassroots organization of determined citizens established the Northwest Community Library on the corner of Poss and Evers Roads in a modular realty office leased from Ray Ellison Industries. Later, the building was donated to the city. As the usage of the library grew, a new larger library was needed. Mayor Irene Baldridge and the Friends of the Leon Valley Public Library, under the leadership of Fay Schneider and Dr. Martin Meltz, were instrumental in the fundraising for the new facility. It was built in 1992 by the City of Leon Valley Public Works Department and is located at 6425 Evers Road. It was renamed the Leon Valley Public Library.

Leon Valley has continued to enrich the quality of its peoples' lives. Contained within the city limits of three and a half square miles are the following: the 24-acre Raymond Rimkus Park, offering tennis courts, soccer fields, a baseball diamond, children's playground, and walking paths; the 36-acre Huebner-Onion Natural Area with primitive walking trails; a community center; a conference center; and two swimming pools.

Leon Valley strives to preserve its autonomy, small-town atmosphere, and unique heritage. Together with a team of architects, it has developed plans for a town center, beautification programs, and other rejuvenation projects. By honoring the past and enjoying the present, Leon Valley is building for the future.

One

EARLY SETTLEMENT

The first settlers from Germany and Austria brought with them old-world traditions. Some settlers came with skills, such as blacksmithing, furniture making, and metalworking. The women churned butter, made lye soap, and sometimes wove their own cloth. Water was carried from springs or streams and pumped from the well by a windmill into a storage tank. Because there were few doctors, the families used many home remedies. Oil imported from Germany called Lebenswecken was used as an ointment. *Versprecht* (to speak) was also used, and a person with the power to versprecht would lightly rub a wound in a circular motion and whisper a secret saying. This ability was passed from one generation to the next and was usually possessed by women. As a matter of survival, nothing was wasted, and the families often shared their resources. Most families had milk cows, chickens, turkeys, and hogs. They grew vegetables, cotton, wheat, corn, oats, and cane. When butchering a hog, the only things that were disposed of were bones and hair. The hogs furnished casings for sausage, fat to make soap, bacon, ham, brains, and cracklings. Pomace was made from meat juices, meat, spices, and corn meal. The children usually had animal traps set and caught opossums, raccoons, foxes, skunks, and ringtail cats. They skinned them, dried the skins, and sold them.

Fredrich "Fritz" Bormann came to the United States in 1856 as a young man of 21 years. Six years later, he enlisted in the Union army and was wounded twice. In 1869, he married Katherine Schoen in San Antonio. They established a farm near what is now Poss Road. (Courtesy of K&EAHC.)

Katherine Schoen Bormann was born in New Braunfels, Texas, in 1845. She gave birth to 10 children, Dedloff, Lena, Francis, Fred, William, Elisa, Katharina, Dora, Arthur, and Heinrich. Three of the children died before the age of four. All of the children and their spouses are buried at Zion Lutheran Cemetery, with the exception of Arthur and his wife. (Courtesy of K&EAHC.)

10

Heinrich Steubing Sr. married Katherine Wetz. They had six children. Katherine died after the birth of her last child, and Heinrich remarried. He is shown here with his children. Pictured from left to right are (seated) Anna Steubing Reininger, Heinrich Steubing Sr., Katherine Steubing Reininger, and Emma Steubing Reininger; (standing) Karl Steubing, Sylvester Steubing, and Heinrich "Henry" Steubing Jr. The three daughters married Reininger men from a neighboring farm. The Steubing farm was beside Leon Creek at Bandera Road and Eckert Roads. They grew sorghum cane and owned a sorghum molasses press and cooking vat, which was used by many families in the community. Water was pumped from the well by a windmill into a storage tank. If there was no wind, there was no water, so water had to be conserved. Saturday was bath day, when water was heated on the woodstove and the bath was taken in a washtub. In the summer, the children bathed under the outside hydrant. (Courtesy of Gloria Anderson.)

Heinrich "Henry" Steubing Jr. married Frances Bormann in 1896. They lived on a homestead near Leon Creek and raised nine children. He is shown here seated and smiling on the occasion of his 81st birthday on May 27, 1953, surrounded by his children. Pictured from left to right are Dorothy Steubing Tietze, Richard Steubing, Hilda Steubing Hand, Raymond Steubing, Ottilie Steubing Belzung, Johnny Steubing, Ada Steubing Krueger, Emanuel Steubing, and Ella Steubing Nickel. Primarily a farmer, Steubing also was an accomplished carpenter who helped build Zion Lutheran Church in Helotes. He loved music and played the violin and several brass instruments. His music was well known at the Hermann Sons Hall on Braun Road. Steubing believed in education and helped found Evers School, the first school in Leon Valley. He served on the first public school board established in Leon Valley in 1924. (Courtesy of Gloria Anderson.)

Heinrich and Clara Voges Poss owned and operated a working farm on the land now known as Grass Valley and Pavona Place. Part of their farm included the land on which the Leon Valley Elementary School is located. It is now owned by the Fryer and Poss families on Huebner Road. (Courtesy of Barbara Fryer.)

Schwarz & Bangert, Photographers, New Braunfels, Texas.

Tekla Poss built the small-framed house on Strawflower Road for her aging parents, Heinrich and Clara Poss, in the late 1940s. Her brother Charlie Poss Sr. and his family moved into the homestead near what is now the Grass Valley Pool. At the death of her parents, Tekla moved into the small-framed house. She later sold the land she inherited from her father, which is now Pavona Place. (Courtesy of Barbara Fryer.)

Andres Salazar was born in the Helotes area in 1895. He married Felipa Camacho in 1918 and moved to the Leon Valley area. At first they lived in the Onion home, where it is said Salazar killed 65 to 70 rattlesnakes. Later, they built their own home near Poss Road, where they raised seven children. Andres Salazar was a farmer but was also recognized for his proficiency in building trades, especially masonry. His sons built the rockwork for the sign at Raymond Rimkus Park. He and his sons constructed many of the early stone homes and other buildings in the area. The Salazar family made possible the Northwest Little League, which was first named Salazar Park. Andres Salazar died in 1984, having been the longest resident in Leon Valley. (Courtesy of K&EAHC.)

Pictured here is the farm home where Gerald Miller and Helen Harrison Miller began their life together in 1928, after Gerald became manager of the 333-acre Fairland Hills dairy farm upon the retirement of his father. The farm was owned by Dr. Pat Nixon and was located on Braun and Bandera Roads, where Camino Bandera, Braun Station, and a service station are now located. (Courtesy of Carol Poss.)

Seated on the front steps of this farm home are members of the family who lived and worked on the farm. From left to right, they are Henry Miller and his sons Leslie Miller and Gerald Miller. Jayne Miller, the youngest daughter, attended Leon Valley Elementary School and taught at that school for a few years after high school graduation. (Courtesy of Carol Poss.)

These silos are still standing on a vacant lot on Huebner Road just off Evers Road. The date they were built is unavailable. Paul Steurenthaler married Katharine Reininger, daughter of Alfred Reininger and Antoinette Evers, so it can be assumed Paul and Katherine were also farmers since the Evers and Reininger farms were nearby. (Courtesy of LVHS.)

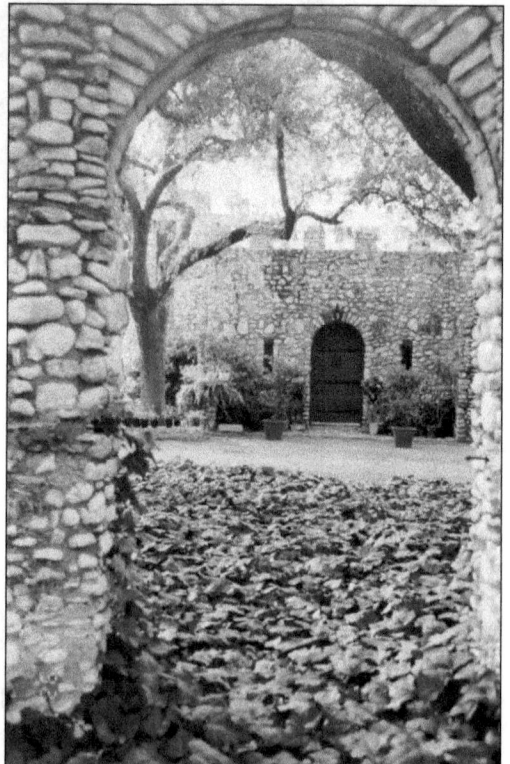

This lovely rock home sits on a hill overlooking Leon Valley and has been referred to as the Castle. Built in 1892, it was occupied by Mary Anita Bonner and her sister Erma in 1929. Mary Anita was an artist of international renown who gave exhibitions of her art in several Texas cities and also in Paris, France. (Courtesy of K&EAHC.)

16

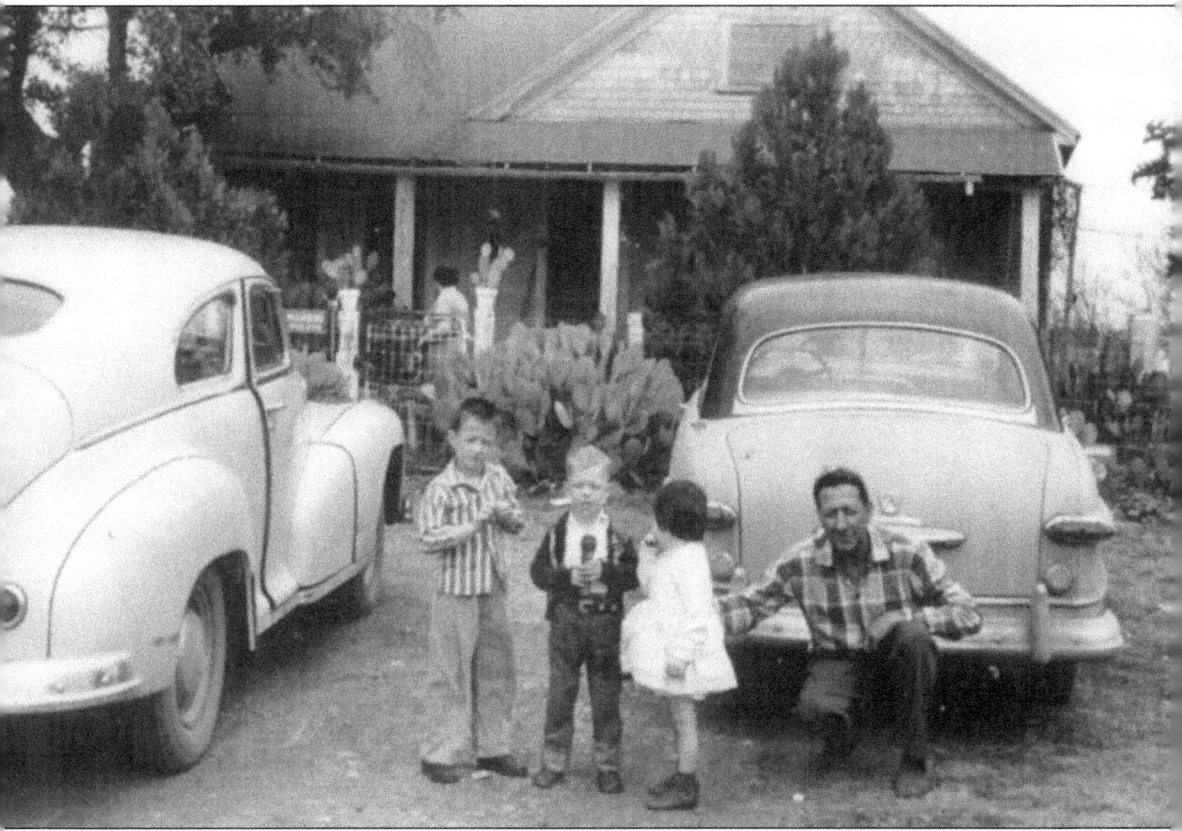

Pictured here are Charlie E. Poss Sr. and three of his grandchildren in the 1950s. From left to right, Dan Poss, Richard Fryer Jr., and Geri Poss are shown in front of the house that was once located close to the Grass Valley swimming pool. On the porch is Barbara Shiner Poss, the children's grandmother. Heinrich and Clara Poss, Charlie's parents, bought the old Bormann homestead and land from Freidrich Bormann's son Arthur in 1922. Two rooms of the house had rock masonry walls that were two- to three-feet thick. There was also a large barn, a windmill, and a food cellar. When the elder Poss couple moved to the small house on Strawflower Road, their son Charlie E. Poss Sr. and his family lived in the homestead until the mid-1960s, when Grass Valley was built and the house was demolished. (Courtesy of Barbara Fryer.)

Christian Evers and his wife, Christine Buck Evers, are shown in this undated photograph. Christian Evers, son of Claus and Johanna Bocken Evers, immigrated to Texas on the *Gutenberg* from Germany in 1885 with his parents and sister Christina. He bought 211 acres in the northwest corner of Huebner and Evers Roads for $3 an acre. (Courtesy of Virginia Evers.)

Six of Christina Evers Wehmeyer Braendle's children are shown in this photograph. Her first husband, Frank Wehmeyer, died three days after their third child was born. She married Christian Braendle the following year. Pictured are, from left to right, Emil Wehmeyer, Gus Braendle, Oscar Braendle, Edward Braendle, and Otto Wehmeyer. (Courtesy of Donna Christopher.)

Taken in 1899 in front of the Claus Evers homestead, this photograph shows Claus Evers, third row, fourth from left, and his son Christian Evers, third row, sixth from the left. Johanna Bocken Evers is in the second row, fourth from left, and her daughter Christine Buck Evers is sixth from left in the second row. Christian Evers and his wife, Christine, had 10 children—Anna, Katherine, Johanna, Bertha, Antoinette, Hartwig, Sabastian, Claus, Mary Helen, and Christian Conrad. The other members of the group include husbands, wives, and children of the Christian Evers family. It appears that the same fabric was used in some of the women's and girls' dresses. They could have been made from feed sack cloth (which was often utilized) or a large bolt of fabric bought from the general store. Christian Evers donated two acres of land for the Evers School, the first school in Leon Valley, built in 1894 at the corner of Evers and Huebner Roads. (Courtesy of Virginia Evers.)

In 1928, these six children happily relaxed on the Henry Steubing farm on a bright sunny day. Pictured from left to right are (first row) Dorothy Steubing, Elton Steubing, and Clarence Steubing; (second row) Richard "Sonny" McCullough, Frances Steubing, and Muriel Steubing. (Courtesy of Gloria Anderson.)

The back of this photograph states, "Come on; get the faucets turned on Eddie." The Edward Anderson family was living on Sawyer Road in Leon Valley in 1944 at the time this photograph was taken. This just goes to show that milk does not originate at the super market as some of today's schoolchildren may think. (Courtesy of Gloria Anderson.)

Joseph Huebner emigrated from Austria in March 1853 with his wife, Caroline, and two children, Anna and Franz. In 1858, he purchased land 10 miles northwest of San Antonio and, over the next 20 years, purchased additional land, making him the owner of over 800 acres in what is now Leon Valley, Texas. He began his ranching and stagecoach stop operations while building his herds of cattle, mules, and horses. His stop provided a watering hole, blacksmith services, change of stock (if needed), and overnight accommodations (if the creek was impassable). This early photograph shows four generations of the Huebner family. Pictured from left to right are Anna Huebner Henson (1846–1926), George Henson (standing), Caroline Huebner (1826–1923), and Gladys Henson Royal, holding her children Helen and Gilbert. (Courtesy of K&EAHC.)

□ HOMES
𝕏𝕏𝕏 DIRT ROAD
- - BOUNDRY
～～ CREEK
( ) NEXT OWNER

BABCOCK ROAD
George Reininger

N
W ⊕ E
S

Henry Reininger
(Waltisperger)

Ehrler

Ferdernand
Eckart
(Harry
Steubing)

Henry
Steubing Sr.
(Henry
Steubing Jr)

Evers
School-

Evers
Cemetery

Christian Evers

Fritz Bormann
(Fred & Arthur Borman)

Olin &
Arthur
Kneupper

Joseph
Huebner
(Cnign)

John
Hein

Henry
Reining

BANDERA ROAD

Dr.
Monarch
(David
Hunter)

Charles Steubing

Fritz Bormann
(Dedloff Bormann)

Ferdernand
Eckart

Alfred
Reininger

To
Guilbeau
Ranch

BRAUN RD.

LEON CREEK

HUEBNER
CREEK

CULEBRA RD.

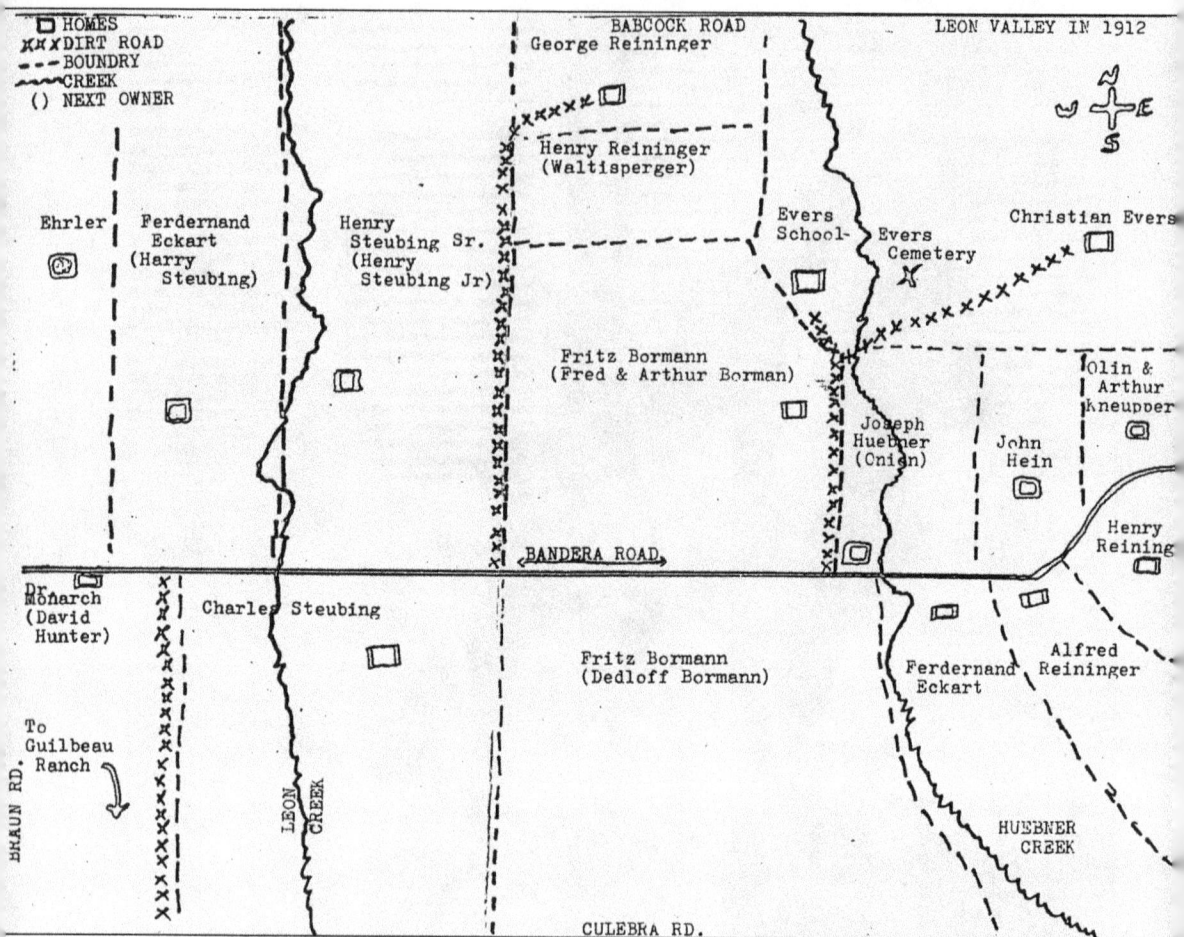

This hand-drawn map indicates the farms and ranches in Leon Valley in 1912. The original boundaries being considered for the city of Leon Valley were the following: the center of Callaghan Road west to the center of Babcock Road, north to the center of Leon Creek, and south down to the center of Acme Road and back to Callaghan Road. When the City of Leon Valley incorporated in 1952, the founding fathers decided the present boundaries, enclosing three and a half miles, were all that the city could provide services for. Leon Valley is surrounded by San Antonio, but in the early days a much larger area on all sides of the current boundaries was called Leon Valley. By 1930, Bandera Road, which had its beginning as a makeshift road for the travel of Indians, wagoneer supplies, and stagecoaches had become graveled from west of Helotes to Bandera. (Courtesy of K&EAHC.)

In 1930, Judge John F. "Pete" Onion purchased 13.82 acres in Leon Valley, which included the house and outbuildings of the Joseph Huebner homestead. Later, he purchased additional acreage. As the family spent more and more time at the property, their love for the homestead grew and they decided to make it their permanent residence. (Courtesy of Linda Persyn.)

Harriet Onion (shown here), Judge Onion, and their five-year-old twin boys, John Jr. and James, took possession of the homestead on April 30, 1930. They all loved the country life and added on to the existing structure to accommodate their family's needs. Harriet Onion was a beloved substitute schoolteacher in Leon Valley. (Courtesy of Frank Onion.)

This is an early map showing the Huebner Settlement along Bandera Road, which was named after Joseph Huebner. The settlement later became part of Leon Valley. In 1930, the Huebner homestead became the residence of Judge John F. Onion and his family. (Courtesy of K&EAHC.)

The twin sons of Judge John F. Onion followed in their father's footsteps and served with the Bexar County District Attorney's office in the early 1950s. Both John Onion Jr., shown on the right, and James Onion were elected to the same criminal district court on which their father had served. (Courtesy of Frank Onion.)

Dr. Pat Ireland Nixon (1883–1965), a prominent San Antonio physician and medical historian, owned a 333-acre farm on Bandera and Braun Roads from 1920 until his death. His son Thomas continued to run the farm until 1972. Many gold medal prize-winning bulls and Jersey cows were raised on the farm. One of the libraries at the University of Texas Health Science Center is named in honor of Dr. Nixon. (Courtesy of Grace Nixon.)

Olive Read Nixon (1886–1964), wife of Dr. Nixon, gave birth to four sons. The two eldest sons, Pat Ireland Nixon Jr. and Robert Nixon, became physicians like their father. All four sons served in World War II. The two youngest sons, Ben and Thomas, were twins. (Courtesy of Grace Nixon.)

This charming photograph of Henry Steubing's four children was taken in the early 1900s at a professional studio. They are, from left to right, Hilda, Ottilie "Tillie," and Richard with Ella standing in the back. (Courtesy of Dorothy Steubing Wright.)

Dr. Pat Ireland Nixon is pictured on his farm with three of his sons in 1932. Ben Nixon, with the cap on, is seated on the car bumper with his first killed deer. Ben's twin brother, Thomas Nixon, is seated next to him. Dr. Nixon is standing at the left and his son Robert Nixon is on the right. (Courtesy of Grace Nixon.)

Thomas and Ben Nixon caught two skunks on their father's farm in this 1927 photograph. Dr. Nixon surgically deodorized them and kept them as pets. On the back of the picture, they had written "our skunks." (Courtesy of Grace Nixon.)

In the days before tricycles came with rubber tires, Ben and Thomas Nixon pose in front of the woodpile on their Fairland Hills farm home in the early 1920s. Ben grew up to be a pilot, and Thomas managed the farm after his father retired. (Courtesy of Grace Nixon.)

These children enjoyed the farm life in the Leon Valley area in the 1930s. The above photograph shows two of the Miller girls, with Betty on the left and Carol on the right. They are riding their tricycles beside their cousin Leslie "Sonny" Miller, who is in his little red wagon. The photograph below shows Betty Miller pulling her baby sister Carol in a makeshift wagon made from a wooden apple crate. The Miller family lived and worked on Dr. Nixon's farm from the late 1920s into the 1930s. Dr. Nixon delivered both girls at their grandmother's home in San Antonio. (Both, courtesy of Carol Poss.)

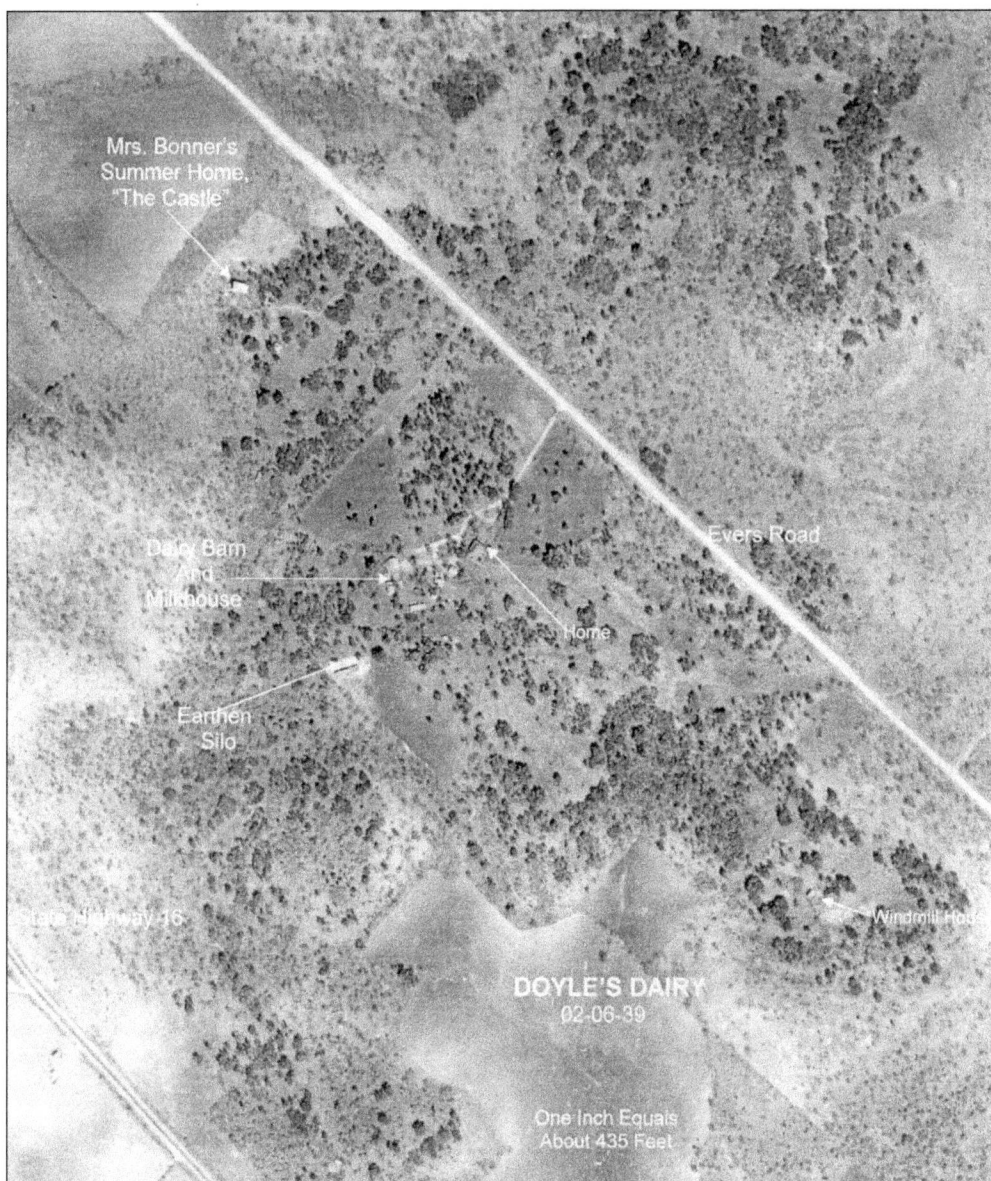

This aerial photograph taken February 6, 1939, shows the Joe Doyle dairy in an area of Leon Valley between Evers Road and State Highway 16 (Bandera Road). The caption states, "One Inch Equals About 435 Feet." The windmill house is shown on the lower right. There is an earthen silo at center left and a dairy barn and milk house in the center of the photograph. The Doyle homestead is in the center just to the right of the dairy barn and milk house. At the upper left corner of the photograph is the summer home known throughout Leon Valley as the Castle, located in what would become the subdivision of Castle Estates. Joe Doyle's brother Bob owned a home on the corner of Poss and Bandera Roads. (Courtesy of Bob Doyle.)

Pictured in this 1941 photograph in front of a dairy barn are three descendents of Henry Steubing, who was an early settler of Leon Valley. The Steubing dairy was located on Bandera and Eckhert Roads. Pictured from left to right are Steubing's first great-grandchild David Anderson, La Nell Tietza, and William Tietze (his arm around the calf's neck). La Nell and William were both grandchildren of Henry Steubing. (Courtesy of Dorothy Steubing Wright.)

This very early Ford automobile belonged to Eddie Anderson's brother. On the back of the photograph is written "My Ford coupe, 1924 Model T, family car." The Model T Ford was known as the "Tin Lizzie" and was the first automobile mass produced on an assembly line. (Courtesy of Gloria Anderson.)

Two

SCHOOLS

Children of the early settlers walked seven or eight miles to school in the town of Helotes. As the number of children increased, the need for a local school became evident. In 1894, the settlers established Evers School on Evers and Huebner Roads. It was a private school for the first two years. The one-room school was constructed from 1-inch-by-10-inch rough boards. In later years, metal siding was put over the boards, and it became known as the Old Tin School. The building was approximately 30 feet by 24 feet and had no ceiling. There were eight grades, and children who wanted to further their education attended high school in San Antonio. In 1924, a public school was built on Bandera and Grissom Roads and named Leon Valley School. Rural school districts in Bexar County consolidated in 1949 to become Northside Consolidated School District No. One. This district eventually became known as the Northside Independent School District. Northside High School, later renamed John Marshall High School, was built on Eckhert Road, graduating its first class of seven students in 1951. In the early 1990s, two new Northside Schools were named after early settlers, Henry Steubing and Christian Evers. Since these early beginnings, the Northside Independent School District has grown to become the fourth largest school district in Texas.

In the mid-1800s, the children of Leon Valley attended school in Helotes. As Leon Valley grew, the need for a local school became evident. In 1894, through the efforts of early settlers, a one-room, wooden schoolhouse, Evers School, was built on the east corner of Evers and Huebner Roads. In 1924, it was moved by tractor to Bandera and Grissom Roads. (Courtesy of K&EAHC.)

The beginning of Texas Independence from Mexico is marked by the annual Battle of Flowers parade in San Antonio. In this early-1900s photograph, the children pictured from left to right with this Leon Valley School float are (first row) Gus Benke, Jesse Richardson, Dorothy Steubing, Robert Brauchle, George Reininger, and J.C. Lackey; (second row) Charles Kuhn, Joe Waller, and Sam Moore. (Courtesy of Clarence Steubing.)

This delightful picture taken in the early 1900s shows Herbert Reininger astride a donkey in front of a silo and a windmill. Many years later as an adult, Herbert told a bridge partner that he always tied his donkey right outside the Leon Valley schoolhouse so that when it "passed gas," it would blow in through the window. (Courtesy of K&EAHC.)

The second school in Leon Valley was built on Bandera Road in 1924 and was called the Leon Valley School. It was renamed Mackey School some time later. The building now houses the Northside Independent School District Learning Center and Museum. A new Leon Valley Elementary School was built on Huebner Road in 1979. (Courtesy of K&EAHC.)

These girls from Evers School are all dressed up and form a drill team. Pictured around 1921 are, from left to right, (first row) teacher Hilda Simmingler, Tyson Dorothy Voight, Vera Steubing, Adela Bormann, and Mildred Steubing; (second row) Ada Steubing, Hedwig Menn, Salema Krueger, and Katy Reininger. (Courtesy of Gloria Anderson.)

Leon Valley School entered a Ford Model T truck covered with live flowers in the 1929 San Antonio annual Battle of Flowers during the fiesta parade. The people in the truck are unidentified. There is no information on whether or not it won a prize. Gloria Anderson believes the theme was the "Capture of Santa Anna." (Courtesy of Gloria Anderson.)

In front of Leon Valley School, around 1934, this lovely all-girl choral group is wearing lavender organdy blouses, headpieces, and white skirts. Only the first row was able to be identified. They are, from left to right, Frances Steubing, Winifred Calvert, Margie Hay, Anita Lux, June Lackey, Dorothy Earhart, Ella Mae Krause, Myra Lee Hay, and Margaret Lackey. (Courtesy of Gloria Anderson.)

These two boys, Raymond Steubing (left) and his classmate ? Decker, are dressed in the Leon Valley School baseball uniforms in the 1930s. They are shown leaning on the fence in front of one of the many farms in the Leon Valley area. (Courtesy of Dorothy Steubing Wright.)

These bathing beauties of the early 1930s show that all their time was not spent on farm labor or school work. Posing on this old Ford car are, from left to right, Clarence Steubing, Gloria McCulloch, Richard McCulloch, Vera Steubing, and Elton Steubing. (Courtesy of Dorothy Steubing Wright.)

These smiling children are in a class at the Leon Valley School in 1927. From left to right, they are (first row) Gloria McCulloch, Myra Lee Hay, Margie Hay, Edna Ebert, and Ruth Reininger; (second row) Rebecca Schmitt, Mary Reininger, Blanch Schmitt, Lorraine Braun, and Dorothy Steubing; (third row) three unidentified boys. (Courtesy of Dorothy Steubing Wright.)

36

This girls' volleyball team is standing in front of Leon Valley School in 1931. From left to right, they are (first row) Katy ?, Dorothy Steubing, two unidentified, principal and coach Terrell Gates; (back row) teacher Annie Akin, Thelma Lynd, Gloria McCullough, Evelyn Patterson, Berta Sales, and unidentified. (Courtesy of Dorothy Steubing Wright.)

Northside High School was built in 1950, and its first senior class had seven students who graduated in 1951. The name was changed in the 1960s to John Marshall High School. The graduates shown here are, from left to right, Geraldine Steubing, George Owen, Carmen Ledesma, Jeanne Loessberg, Doris Voight, Bobbie Hay, and Winifred Wood. (Courtesy of Geraldine Steubing.)

The seventh Pioneer Day was called the "Leon Valley Elementary School Marker Dedication" and was held on April 26, 1981. It honored and commemorated the history of the Leon Valley Elementary School, from its inception as the Evers School in 1894 to its dedication of the commemorative marker and sundial at the new Leon Valley Elementary School on Huebner Road. Pictured above are a few alumni of Leon Valley Elementary School, and they are, from left to right, (first row) Jerry Lynd, Margie Ruempel, Gloria McCulloch, J.C. Lackey, Margaret Lackey, Dorothy Steubing, Frances Steubing, Muriel Steubing, and teacher Terrell Gates; (second row) Robert Brauchle, Lucille Ruempel, Ruth Reininger, Robert Lynd, Charles Kuhn, and Evelyn Patterson. The marker and sundial are shown at left. (Both, courtesy of K&EAHC.)

Ed Cody, superintendent of Northside Independent School District and former principal of Leon Valley Elementary School, addresses the attendees at the dedication ceremony. The procession in the lawn, where attendees viewed the sundial and plaque, was led by Leon Valley Cub Scout Pack 484. (Courtesy of K&EAHC.)

This group on the lawn of Leon Valley Elementary School views the sundial, which was moved from the original Leon Valley School on Bandera and Grissom Roads. The plaque and sundial were presented to a Mr. Schuback, principal of Leon Valley Elementary School. (Courtesy of K&EAHC.)

One of the schools in the Northside Independent School District named after early Leon Valley settlers is the Christian Evers Elementary School, which is pictured here and was dedicated in 1992. The original 1894 Evers School was established by Sylvester Steubing, Fredrich Bormann, Henry Reininger, and Christian Evers. Christian Evers donated two acres of land for the school. (Courtesy of Carol Poss.)

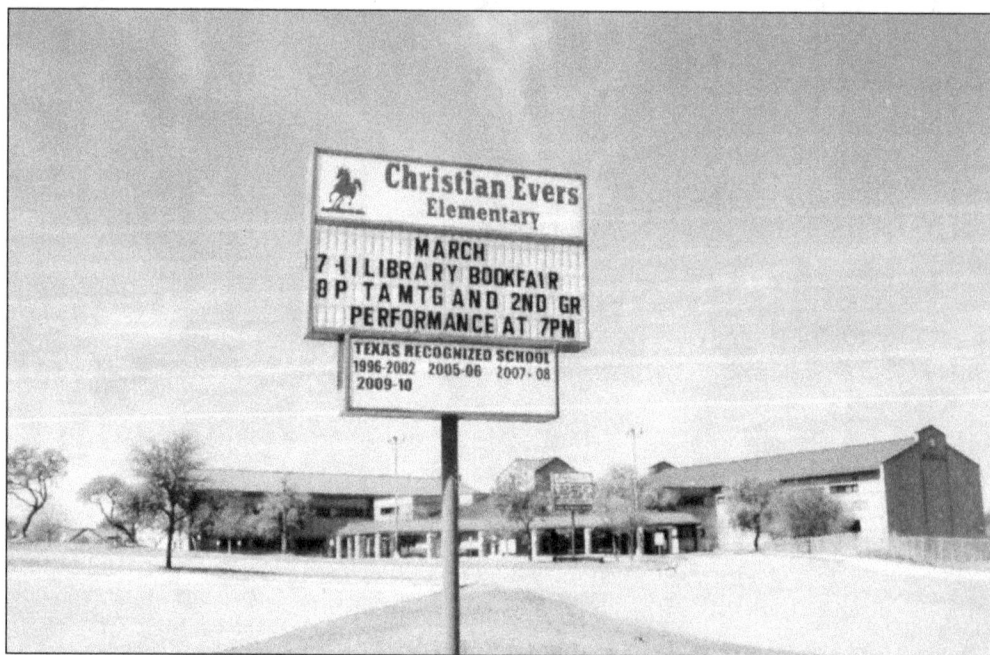

The signpost for the Christian Evers Elementary School is located in front of the school and shows Jack Jordan Middle School in the background, which was named after Jack Jordan, superintendent of schools. Jack Jordan led the dedication of the new Christian Evers Elementary School. (Courtesy of Carol Poss.)

The Henry Steubing Elementary School was built in 1995 by the Northside Independent School District and named after the son of one of the early-1800s Leon Valley settlers, Heinrich Steubing. Heinrich "Henry" Steubing Jr. helped establish a public school in Leon Valley, where he was a member of the first school board. (Courtesy of Carol Poss.)

Pictured here is the newly renovated John Marshall High School auditorium. The grand opening of the auditorium was celebrated on March 3, 2011. The original John Marshall High School was named Northside High School, the first high school in Leon Valley. It graduated its first class of seven students in 1951. (Courtesy of Carol Poss.)

This is the view to the right of the new John Marshall High School auditorium. According to the 1951 high school yearbook, in the beginning of the school's history, their mascot was a goat named "I Can Butt." The goat attended most of their sports events. In all likelihood, the goat came from the developer of Monte Robles Park, Kenneth Haggard, who donated the land for the high school. (Courtesy of Carol Poss.)

Jack Jordan, a leading Texas educator who held the position of superintendent of Northside Independent School District in 1982, is pictured here awarding the Jack Jordan Scholarship Award to Tiffany Fryer at the Northside Activities Center in May 2009. The Jack Jordan Middle School is named in honor of him. (Courtesy of Barbara Fryer.)

Three

EARLY BUSINESSES

Early businesses were established to meet the needs of an expanding population and urbanization. The first store, owned by Joseph and Annie Siedo Dietsch, was located across Bandera Road from Leon Valley School and opened in the early 1920s. It also included their home. Annie Diesch is described as a short, chubby German woman who wore her hair in a bun. The store displayed a glass case with chewing gum and other goodies. Soda water was available in an old-fashioned icebox. Other things for sale were staples, a few canned goods, chicken feed, ready-made bread and pastries, and kerosene. A few years before lunches were provided at the school, students would eat lunch at the store. As automobiles replaced stagecoaches and horses as the main means of transportation, automobile repair shops and gas stations became necessary. A hardware store was established for homeowners, farmers, and ranchers. When butane became available for use as fuel, a butane company was founded. To fill the need for veterinarian services to treat farm and ranch animals, a veterinarian hospital was opened in the Leon Valley area. The first known café not only provided food but also entertainment; it was a meeting place for parties and provided country music for dancing. Many of these businesses are still in existence today.

The Raymond Rimkus Store was the second store in Leon Valley, opening in the late 1930s at the corner of Bandera and Grissom Roads. The original building was of wooden construction. Later, it was rebuilt as a stone structure by local masons and called the Bandera Building. The first door on the left of the building was the entrance to this store. Rimkus brought produce, meat, ice, and other perishables from San Antonio. Various businesses rented out the remainder of the building. Raymond Rimkus was a member of the hastily organized Leon Valley Incorporating Association in 1952 to prevent annexation by the City of San Antonio. He was elected first mayor of Leon Valley, serving from 1957 to 1959. The store hosted the first city council meetings, and most city business was transacted there in the early years of the city. (Courtesy of K&EAHC.)

The 13th Pioneer Day sponsored by the Leon Valley Pageant Association was entitled "Dedication of Raymond Rimkus Store Location Marker." It was held on April 11, 1987, and dedicated a historical marker paid for by Mobil Oil Company, commemorating the location of the Raymond Rimkus Store that was demolished in 1986. (Courtesy of Carol Poss.)

Paula's Café, seen in the center of the photograph, was on the south side of Bandera Road and was about a one-half block from Poss Road. Many residents had a cup of coffee there while waiting for the mail to be delivered on Bandera Road. The rows of mailboxes were across the street from the café. The café was open in the 1940s and 1950s. (Courtesy of K&EAHC.)

The Texas Star Inn was built in 1946 and opened for business under the name of Skinny's Café, which was named after James "Skinny" Norris. Skinny, Kenneth Evers, and Lester Krueger quarried the rock from nearby Leon Creek. The building was erected by the Salazar and Valdez families, who were well-known masons. The building's facade resembles the Alamo. Later, a small patio was added, and many parties were held there. A jukebox provided music for dancing. Skinny and his wife, Rose, were members of the popular bowling league called the Gutter League. In 1952, the café was sold to Frank and Aselee Klein Sr., who renamed it the Texas Star Inn. They enlarged and covered the patio. Many country western musicians played for dances, including Faron Young, Johnny Bush, Ray Price, Ernest Tubb, and Willie Nelson, when he played the fiddle in Ray Price's band. Polly Herchberger and Dodie Sullivan bought the restaurant in 1979 and kept it open for another three years. In 1981, it was purchased by Grady Coward and renamed Grady's BBQ. (Courtesy of K&EAHC.)

The Edward "Eddie" Anderson Garage opened for business in 1946 on Bandera Road, close to Eckert Road. The garage is still in business today. David Anderson, Eddie Anderson's son, managed the garage after Eddie retired. The garage is still a family-owned business. (Courtesy of Gloria Anderson.)

This photograph of the updated Anderson Garage is shown rebuilt and in the same location as the original. From left to right are Gloria Anderson, Eddie Anderson, their son David Anderson and his wife, Beverly. The Anderson Garage celebrated its 65th anniversary in 2011. David is the great-great-grandson of early settler Heinrich Steubing, who came to Leon Valley in the 1800s. This marks David as the fifth generation to own the Steubing property. (Courtesy of David Anderson.)

W.G. "Gus" Meiske Service Station was located at the corner of Bandera and Poss Roads. He bought the station in 1954 and sold it in 1966. His motto was, "Don't Cuss, call Gus." The Meiske family lived in the house to the right of the station. (Courtesy of K&EAHC.)

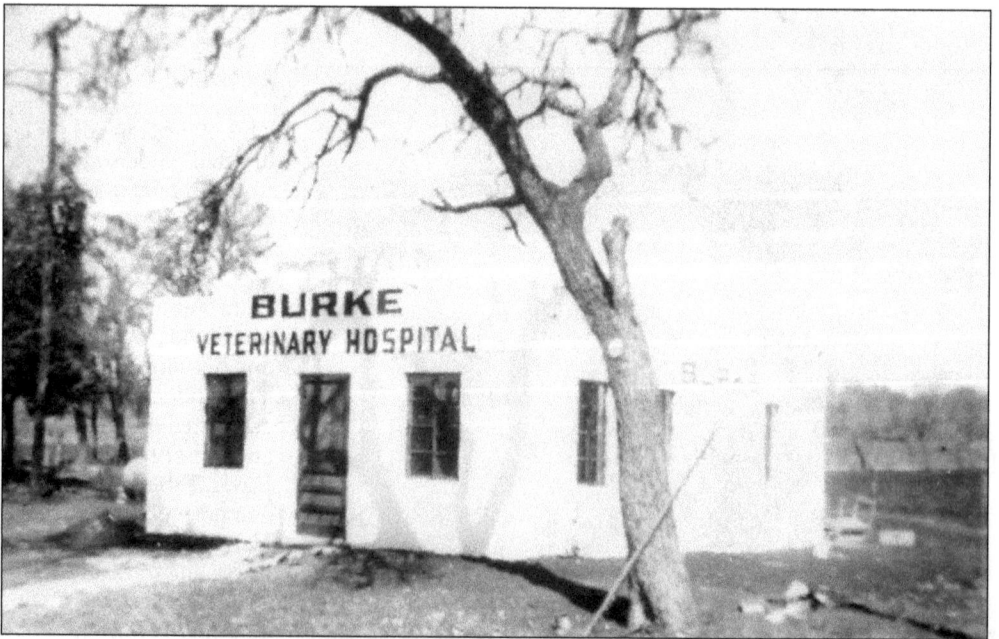

Dr. W.Z. Burke opened his first veterinary hospital on Bandera Road near what is now the subdivision of French Creek. He cared for the animals on 71 of the early farms in Leon Valley and was also an education pioneer. His second office was located on Bandera Road near Loop 410. It is still a veterinary hospital. (Courtesy of W.Z. Burke Elementary School.)

This neon garage sign to the left of the picture was first located at Alton Applewhite's Automotive and Collision Center at his original location on South Flores Street in San Antonio in 1935. After being in business for 39 years, Applewhite's relocated to Leon Valley in the 1970s. (Courtesy of Carol Poss.)

The current Applewhite's Automotive store is located on Bandera Road, next door to the Northside Independent School District Center and Museum. Alton Applewhite flew his own airplane for many years and served in World War II as a flight trainer captain. He passed away in 2006. (Courtesy of Carol Poss.)

Uhl's Storage Company started their business in the 1940s, shortly after World War II. The original Leon Valley airport hangars are part of this facility. The airport was used for training pilots during the war. It was later used for boat storage and repair because it was conveniently located on the way to Medina Lake. (Courtesy of Carol Poss.)

One of the original airport hangars is shown in this photograph, which was taken inside the grounds of the storage facility. Uhl's Storage is located on Grissom Road, a short distance from Bandera Road. The name has recently been changed to Leon Valley Storage. (Courtesy of Carol Poss.)

This early icehouse, known only as Luckey's, was open in the late 1940s and early 1950s and was located on the corner of Bandera and El Verde Roads. A beauty shop operated by the wife of the owner of Luckey's store was located in the Spanish-style building south of where the Leon Valley City Hall is now located. (Courtesy of LVHS.)

Mandry's Hardware Store was located at the corner of Bandera and Poss Roads and was the first store of its kind in the Leon Valley area. Mandry sold hardware, lumber, and feed. Many people frequented the store in the early days of Leon Valley. (Courtesy K&EAHC.)

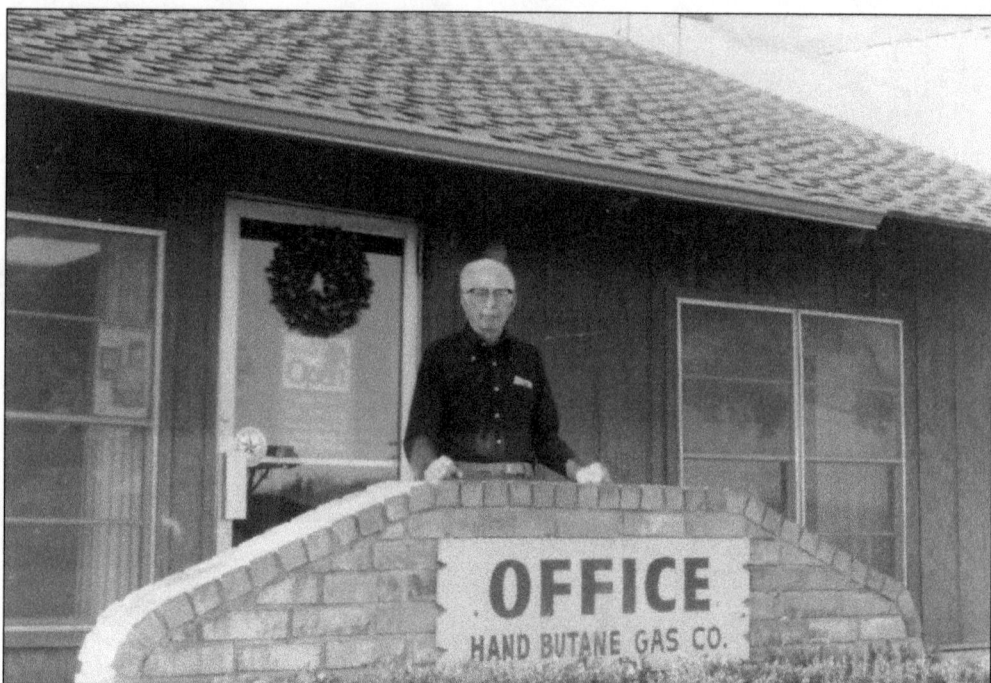

Preston and Hilda Steubing Hand started their Hand Butane Company in 1958 at the east corner of Bandera and Eckhert Roads. They moved their business and home to Helotes, Texas, in 1993. Hilda is one of the descendents of early settler Heinrich Steubing. (Courtesy of Gloria Anderson.)

John and Jill Anderson Kassai opened the Propane Depot on Eckhert Road in January 1994. Another descendent of early settler Heinrich Steubing, Jill is the sixth generation to own this property. She is the granddaughter of Eddie and Gloria Anderson, who opened the Anderson Garage in 1946, and the daughter of David and Beverly Anderson. (Courtesy of Jill Kassai.)

Four

FROM A COMMUNITY
TO A CITY

In the early 1930s, the community was composed of the Leon Valley School, the store across the street, farms, ranches, and a few homes. Resident N.C. Sawyer bought and subdivided 400 acres of land into five-acre and 10-acre tracts, building four framed houses and three rock houses. He named the area as Leon Acres. This first subdivision was located near Sawyer Road. People who bought acreage began to build houses. In the mid-1930s, a great spurt of growth occurred. On March 12, 1952 a newspaper reporter happened to see a map at San Antonio City Hall, which showed that the city council planned to annex Leon Valley. He came out to interview a few people. That was the first anyone had heard of it. City leaders had what they called their "Paul Revere Meeting" because they alerted one another and called a meeting that night. Gathering 133 signatures on a petition, which was taken to the courthouse the next morning, they filed with the Bexar County Judge thwarting the attempt by San Antonio to annex Leon Valley. Leon Valley officially received recognition as a city on March 31, 1952, after the ballots were cast (169 for and 15 against) at the election to incorporate. The city limits consisted of only three and one half square miles because the city leaders wanted to assure adequate services.

Among the many celebrated events in Leon Valley was the dedication of the Leon Valley City Hall on September 26, 1981. Shown here are two scenes of the crowd by the newly completed building. Since these early days, Leon Valley has matured into an exemplary community continuing in the trailblazing legacy of the early settlers with a nationally recognized recycling program (the first in Bexar County), the first to offer Internet access at the library even before San Antonio, and many other "firsts." Continuing to offer quality services for citizens and guests, Leon Valley offers "small-town hospitality and big-city advantages." (Both, courtesy K&EAHC.)

Shown in the above photograph is the original library building, which is now known as the library annex. In 1976, the Leon Valley Development Committee appointed by Mayor Marcus Semmelmann supported the organization of a public library. The library opened with great fanfare in May 1977, checking out 595 items that month. Phil Francis, Dr. Martin Meltz, Fay Snyder, Gladys Nixon, Ken Ward, and many others served in numerous ways to make the Northwest Community Library (later the Leon Valley Public Library) a reality. In 1992, a new library, shown in the photograph below, was built at its present location on 6425 Evers Road in 1992. The library has won many awards; most recently the 2010 Achievement of Excellence in Libraries Award. Only 27 of more than 500 public libraries in Texas have received this award. (Both, courtesy of LVPL.)

How did the library books get from their original home in the library annex to the new library building on Evers Road? The answer is one by one. Each book was carried in the "Great Book Brigade" by faithful friends and volunteers of the library. Evers Road was closed for two hours to facilitate the move. The books were hand carried, carried in bags, and pulled by little red wagons by children. The above photograph shows the return trek back to the annex for more books, and the photograph below shows the library marquee urging participants to "Be Here" for the great event. (Both, courtesy of LVPL.)

Library director Joyce Trent expresses heartfelt thanks to Reed Moore, the assistant director of public works and library project manager, at the completion of the new library building on Evers Road. The completion of the library did, in fact, enable citizens of Leon Valley and the surrounding area to "read more!" (Courtesy of LVPL.)

Standing in front of the donation plaque, which listed contributions by businesses, corporations, and individuals at the library opening, are, from left to right, library director Joyce Trent, founders Barbara Yount and Marion Brekken, and first staff employee Peggy Bissett. (Courtesy of LVPL.)

Marilynn Kinman McCain poses at the opening of the library and the 40th anniversary of the city. It was through the generosity of Marilynn that the city was able to have the available land for the public works department, the conference center, and the community center. She sold the land to the city at a greatly reduced price. (Courtesy of LVPL.)

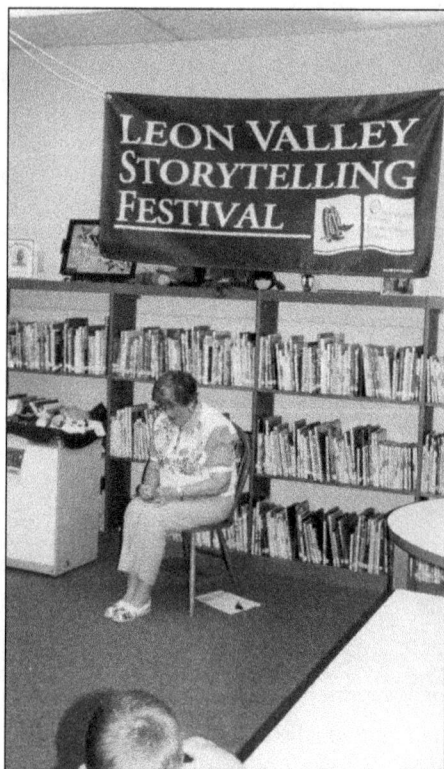

The original children's storyteller for the library was retired librarian Alita Cooper. She still continues in this role and also received an honorary award of Hometown Hero, an award given by Time-Warner Company for outstanding performance by a city volunteer. Her dedication to the children of Leon Valley is exemplary. (Courtesy of LVPL.)

Former mayor Kenneth Alley is shown with the library showcase that was presented to the new library by the Northwest Senior Organization. It was put to good use at the time and has continued to be a delight to library patrons and visitors with various displays. (Courtesy of LVPL.)

Library volunteer Joyce Sefer, shown here on the right, founded the Leon Valley Literacy Program, which was a huge success because many people took advantage of it. The unidentified student shown here was among the first to "graduate." The many volunteers and students who participated gained much in sharing this educational experience. (Courtesy of LVPL.)

On April 9, 1988, the 14th Pioneer Day at the Leon Valley Senior Community Center was sponsored by the City of Leon Valley. The event included the dedication of the building. Mayor Irene Baldridge is standing by the monument in front of the center, which is dedicated "to all those who have served their neighbors, their country, and their God in preservation of our national heritage." (Courtesy of K&EAHC.)

The community center building at the library complex is the host of many activities, including civic and community events, family reunions, and weddings. Ongoing senior activities include exercise classes, line dancing, bridge, dominoes, a monthly senior luncheon, an annual rummage sale, and many others. (Courtesy K&EAHC.)

In 1981, Leon Valley did not have a post office. Shown here is the mobile post office facility that was provided for mailing at Christmastime that year. The city government saw a need to provide local service. A new post office building was estimated to cost over a million dollars. (Courtesy of K&EAHC.)

On October 19, 1985, the new Leon Valley Branch Post Office was dedicated on Huebner Road. Shown here at the podium is postmaster John Saldana. Mayor Irene Baldridge attended the ceremony as well as several members of the Leon Valley Area Business & Professional Association, the court for the Leon Valley Pageant Association, and the Coke Stevenson Middle School band. (Courtesy of K&EAHC.)

The City of Leon Valley public works employees received help in building a pavilion in the city park from the Naval Mobil Construction Battalion No. 22 (Seabees). The Seabees are all wearing white shirts. Mayor Kenneth Alley is shown to the right of the banner. (Courtesy of K&EAHC.)

The Raymond Rimkus Park pavilion is equipped with a large grill, tables, and benches, and it can be reserved for special events. Civic and community celebrations, birthday parties, and other family celebrations as well as field days for local schools and kindergartens are often enjoyed here. (Courtesy of Carol Poss.)

A gathering of mayors is shown in this April 1982 photograph. Shown from left to right, they are Vernon Schuhardt (Leon Valley mayor, 1969–1974), Henry Daughtry (Leon Valley mayor, 1959–1964), Kenneth Alley (Leon Valley mayor, 1980–1984), Charlotte Asch (Leon Valley mayor pro-tem, 1982), Daniel Webster (Balcones Heights mayor), and William Sharp (Shavano Park mayor). (Courtesy of K&EAHC.)

Lions Club members Arthur Browne (left) and Henry Nixon (right) present the US flag to Mayor Kenneth Alley (1980–1984) during this 1980 ceremony at the Municipal Building. The planning and completion of the Municipal Building complex, annexation of Monte Robles Park, the John Marshall High School area, and the Northside School District headquarters took place during Mayor Alley's term in office. (Courtesy K&EAHC.)

The first recycling pickup by "Garbage Gobbler" in Leon Valley occurred in 1988 as a result of volunteer efforts. Shown here are, from left to right, Shirley Kochheiser, member of the recycling committee; Irene Baldridge, Leon Valley mayor; "Captain Waste," of Garbage Gobbler; and Rita Burnside, member of the recycling committee. (Courtesy of Rita Burnside.)

Reminding Leon Valley citizens to keep recycling, this group gathered in November 1996 to install signs around the city. Those identified are Mayor Marcella "Marcy" Meffert (1998–2004, first row, center) in an Earthwise Living shirt, and to her left are library director Joyce Trent, Mary Key, and Rita Burnside. (Courtesy of Rita Burnside.)

The Leon Valley Police Department came into being in the 1970s. Shown here at a celebration of the Ninth Pioneer Day in April 1983, which was sponsored by the Leon Valley Pageant Association, are five of Leon Valley's finest. Before the department was created, a Leon Valley City council member served as police commissioner. (Courtesy K&EAHC.)

This photograph shows the lake that once graced Leon Valley in the area behind the library complex just off Evers Road. It was used for canoeing and fishing by local residents. Filled in by the early 1970s, the space is now occupied by the public works department, the conference center, and the community center. (Courtesy of K&EAHC.)

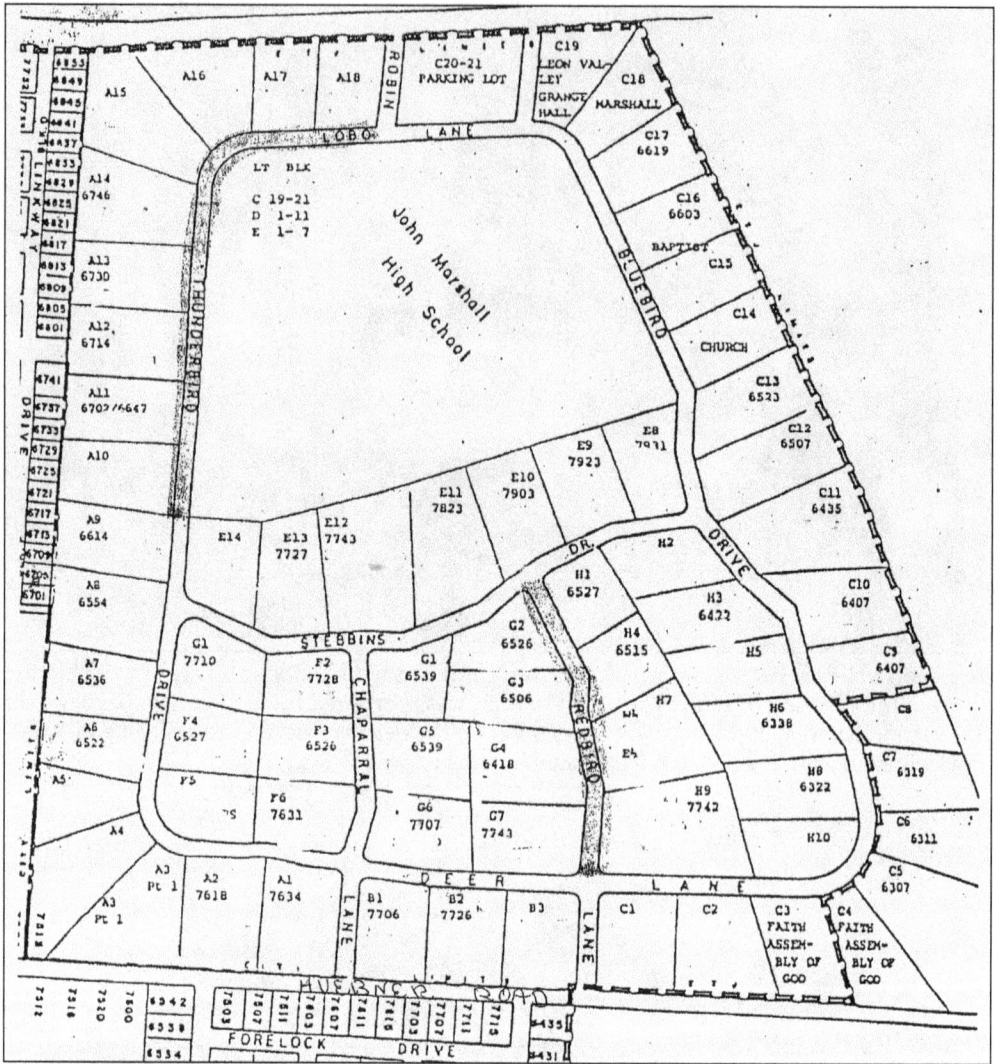

Shown here is a map of Monte Robles Park, an early development north of Huebner Road. In the mid-1940s, three entrepreneurs—Kenneth and Mary Louise Haggard and Mary's father, Harry Stebbins—bought approximately 240 acres of land between Eckhert Road and Huebner Road. They subdivided the land into a neighborhood with large lots and plenty of room for children to play. They plotted the streets in a winding fashion to encourage a safe neighborhood for traffic. At that time, children attended school at the Leon Valley School on Bandera and Grissom Roads but needed to finish their education at San Antonio schools. A high school was needed for the area. In 1949, four school districts joined to form the Northside Rural High School District. Kenneth Haggard and Harry Stebbins donated 16.5 acres for the building, and the Northside High School was built. In the early 1980s, Monte Robles Park and the Northside High School, which is now John Marshall High School, were annexed by Leon Valley. (Courtesy of Horace Staph.)

66

Pictured here is the old entrance to Monte Robles Park. The developers named the streets going in one direction after birds and the ones going the other direction after animals. They wanted one of the streets named "Palamino" because they owned a herd of 150 Palamino horses, but when the City of Leon Valley annexed the subdivision, the name was changed to "Stebbins." This was named after the older developer because San Antonio already had a street named Palamino. Mary Louise Haggard Joseph, the youngest of the developer's seven children, enjoyed telling the following story. She remembers sitting at the dinner table one evening when the phone rang. It was the school's principal who told Kenneth Haggard that he needed to come get his kids out of the school. Haggard saw that all of his children were seated at the table. The principal said he was not talking about his children; he was talking about his goats. Someone had inadvertently left the gate open, and the entire herd of goats was parading down the halls of the school. (Courtesy of Carol Poss.)

Representing Leon Valley at the ribbon-cutting ceremony of the Skaggs Albertson Store on Bandera Road and Loop 410 in 1976 was the Kingsmen, a civic group that bolstered the image of Leon Valley. Pictured from left to right are Mayor Marcus Semmelmann (1974–1978), store director Charles Stephens, and Jack Brannen, King Leo III. The customer in the background is unidentified. (Courtesy of K&EAHC.)

The Kingsmen were available to celebrate many events as well as represent the city as representatives of the Leon Valley Pageant Association. Here, they stand in front of the newly dedicated Raymond Rimkus Park. They were always dressed in bright red jackets, white trousers, and ties. (Courtesy of K&EAHC.)

The Grange Hall on Eckert Road was built and dedicated to serve the needs of the community long before other such facilities were available. A building site of two acres was purchased in 1950, a few feet from the Northside High School. Money was raised by annual carnivals and barbecue dinners. In 1955, the members of the Grange committee purchased a barracks building at Kelly Field and arranged for its removal to the building site. Ten members prepared the slab foundation, lowered the building to the foundation, and bolted it down. Electrical wiring was installed, and hooking up to the school water system was accomplished. Restrooms and a kitchen were furnished. Linoleum was laid, and a septic tank was installed. Leveling and graveling of the grounds were also necessary. Sixty members worked on this project, using a total of 679 man-hours. Total cost of the building was $3,058.67. The boarded up Grange building is still standing. (Courtesy of Carol Poss.)

Shown here demonstrating EMS and fire rescue maneuvers are members of the Leon Valley Fire Department. Looking on are volunteers from various civic organizations and members of a leadership program that was established to acquaint potential city council members with the activities of all city departments. The fire department organizes and conducts educational programs, including home and fire safety, inspections of homes on request, child car seat safety, and many others. They also visit local schools and conduct programs. Located on the city webpage is a link to the fire department and a kids' site with cartoons and games, which teach fire and home safety. Before the fire department was organized, the Bexar County Fire Station handled fires in the area. Their building was located on Bluebird Lane next to the Grange Hall and is still standing. (Courtesy of K&EAHC.)

The "Library Lion" has become a common sight in Leon Valley parades and library programs. He is present at many of the storytelling events and pet parades. Since Leon Valley is known as the "Valley of the Lions," library director Joyce Trent had the costume custom made in the early 1990s to compliment the theme. In the beginning, Trent herself wore the lion costume, and then as her youngest son, Harley, grew tall, he played the lion role. Shown in this decorated silver truck as the Leon Valley Public Library's entry in the Fourth of July Parade are, from left to right, Elisa Magee, her son Christopher Magee, and Harley Trent in the lion's costume. Parades have played a large part in Leon Valley celebrations, beginning in the 1970s with the early Stagecoach Days Parade and continuing with the Fourth of July parades. (Courtesy of LVPL.)

The Kinman House, shown in this photograph, was originally the home of Euel and Marilynn McCain. After McCain died, his widow married William Kinman. Kinman was mayor of Leon Valley from December 1996 until December 1970. He resigned for health reasons and died December 1974. The house was sold in February 2006 to the City of Leon Valley. The Leon Valley Public Works Department filled in the basement, which had been a civil defense shelter and renovated the home as offices. It now houses the City of Leon Valley Economic Development Department. Recently, the Leon Valley Economic Development Corporation was established, which "considers funding for both new facilities and expansion of existing facilities and for the expansion or modernization of existing facilities and structures." The administrative assistant of the economic development department manages the rentals for the community and conference centers. The house also serves as an early voting center during elections. (Courtesy of Carol Poss.)

Five

CELEBRATIONS IN LEON VALLEY

Civic and community events began early in Leon Valley with the formation of the Leon Valley Pageant Association in March 1973. The association's goal was to compile the history of Leon Valley, its citizens, and the surrounding area. The stated functions of the organization were to honor and celebrate the pioneers of Leon Valley with an annual event and designate and maintain historical sites. Records of these events are archived in the Kenneth and Esther Alley Historic Collection housed in the Leon Valley Public Library. Incorporated as a Texas nonprofit organization, the pageant association continues today under the name of the Leon Valley Historical Society. Among the many activities the early Leon Valley Pageant Association sponsored were the following: an annual Stagecoach Days Parade, dedication of monuments throughout the city, recognition of early pioneers and the town's Indian heritage, and honoring the various city departments, schools and students, churches, and civic leaders. One of the main goals of the Leon Valley Historical Society is to preserve the Huebner-Onion Homestead and Stagecoach Stop and develop it as a living history museum and nature center for the benefit of schoolchildren, citizens, and tourists. The society has held many fundraising events and celebrations to help preserve the old stagecoach stop. Annual fundraising dinners with a silent auction, garage sales, and the selling of stagecoach prints by a well-known artist as well as grant writing helped preserve the buildings.

Shown here is the first Queen of Leon Valley, Nancy Fryer, at the beginning of the Stagecoach Days celebration in 1972, which was sponsored by the Leon Valley Pageant Association. It was the first attempt to bring people together at an event that would be fun and also celebrate the history and heritage of Leon Valley. By May 1975, the event had grown to a three-day festival, including a parade down Evers Road from Huebner Road to Bandera Road. Booths were lined up along the route and a carnival was in full swing. Free shows featuring bands, dancing, gymnastics, gun fighters, bands, fiddle playing, and elementary school choirs were among the events offered. Marching down Evers Road on that Saturday were 66 parade entrants, including marching bands, floats, Leon Valley city officials, honor guards, clowns, the Sheriff's Jr. Mounted Posse, bike riders, the Leon Valley float with the queen and her court, and a Leon Valley fire truck. (Courtesy of Nancy Fryer Turner.)

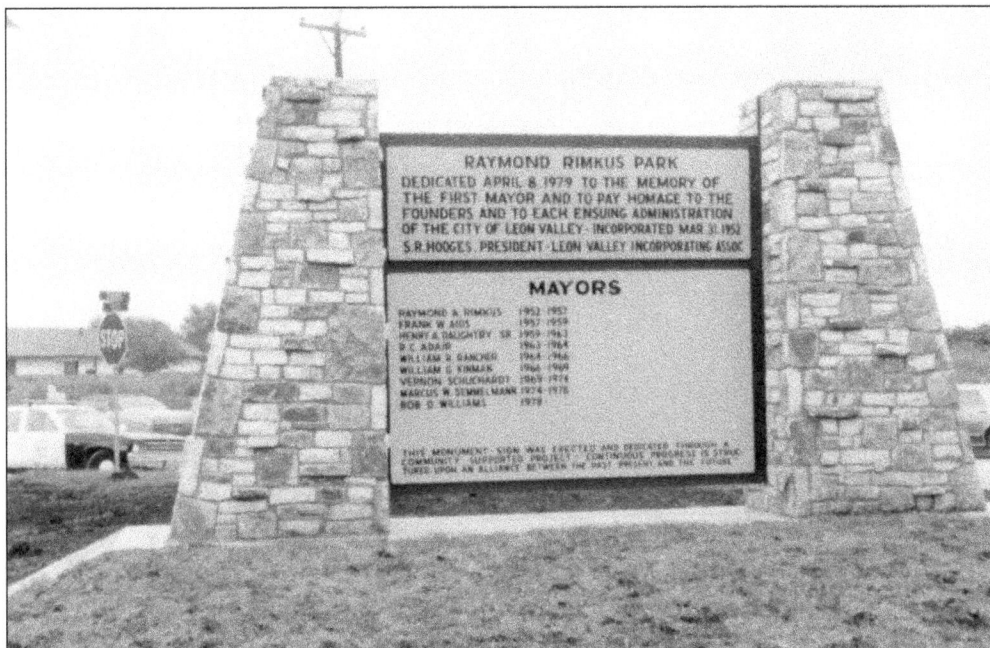

The Raymond Rimkus Park monument and sign were dedicated on April 8, 1979, the Fifth Pioneer Day, to the memory of the founding mayor, Raymond Rimkus, and to pay homage to the founders and to each ensuing administration of the City of Leon Valley. The sign contains the names of the mayors serving up until the time of the dedication. (Courtesy of K&EAHC.)

Margo Salazar, one of the sons of the Andres Salazar family who were early pioneers of Leon Valley, stands in front of the Evers Road side of the Raymond Rimkus Park monument. Andres and his sons were masons for many of the buildings in Leon Valley. (Courtesy of K&EAHC.)

Rita Burnside started the annual Pet Parade in 1989. This starting lineup of children and their pets was taken on the lawn in front of the community center in 1993. Each pet receives an award for longest tail, smallest dog, and so forth. (Courtesy of Rita Burnside.)

At the 1991 annual Pet Parade, refreshments were shared at a party for children and their parents at the Raymond Rimkus Park pavilion across Evers Road from the Leon Valley Public Library. Children are taught responsible pet care as part of this celebration. Pets may include gerbils, hamsters, lizards, snakes, and other unusual animals. (Courtesy of Rita Burnside.)

"Snow Day," at the proposed site of the library expansion, was the kick-off event for fundraising for the children's wing of the library. On December 2, 2006, many pounds of crushed ice were sprayed on the area to make snow. (Courtesy of LVPL.)

As the sign says, "Snow is here today, gone tomorrow but the children's wing will be here always!" Many of Leon Valley's children had never seen snow. It was a new, exciting, and cold adventure for them. Mittens were available as well as hot chocolate and cookies. (Courtesy of LVPL.)

This photograph, taken on the proposed site of the children's wing addition to the Leon Valley Public Library, shows crushed ice being sprayed to make snow. Children and adults all had a cold and glorious time. The children's wing will add much needed space to the present library. (Courtesy Sherry Watson.)

In the Leon Valley Community Center on this festive evening, the annual Holiday Concert plays to a full-capacity crowd. This event began in the early 1900s and features local school bands and children's choirs. A Christmas tree lighting ceremony is also held. (Courtesy of Rita Burnside.)

The annual Breakfast with Santa event has been held the first Saturday in December for over 22 years. Pictured here with Santa (alias Reuben Madrid) is Lydia Lerma, who has been coming to the event since early childhood. Photographs are taken of each child and enclosed in a decorative holiday frame to be taken home. (Courtesy of LVPL.)

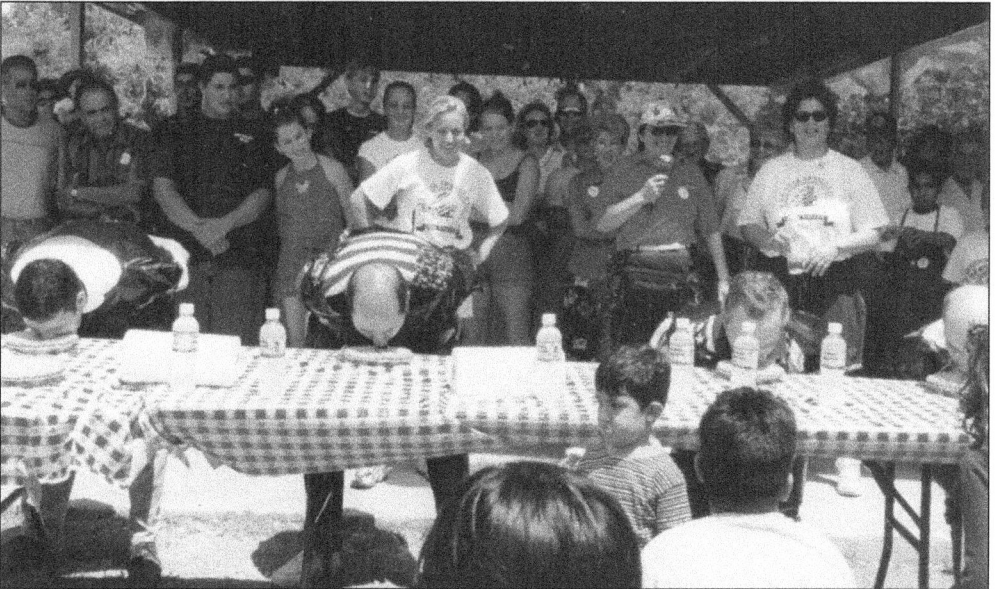

At a fun Fourth of July event in the late 1990s, Mayor Marcy Meffert, with microphone, presides over city council members and the city manager in a pie-eating contest. Taken at the pavilion in the park, this photograph shows that in Leon Valley, city officials believe in facing issues head on. (Courtesy of LVPL.)

The clowns pictured here are entertaining the children with balloon animals and magic tricks at the Breakfast with Santa annual event in 2006. This celebration is sponsored by the Friends of the Leon Valley Public Library more as a "fun-raising" than fundraising event. The event began with pancake breakfasts made by volunteers. Now, however, breakfast tacos, coffee, hot chocolate, fruit cups, orange juice, doughnuts, and *buñuelos* (fried dough balls) are sold. A companion to Breakfast with Santa is the silent auction called Leon Noël, where patrons bid on donated items during the festivities. Entrance is free, and food tickets are sold. Several craft tables by local vendors and a craft table sponsored by the Friends of LVPL are part of the program. It is the first community event of the Christmas season, preceding the Christmas Concert and Christmas Tree Lighting event. The public works department and the civic affairs committee of the city decorate the community center. (Courtesy of Sherry Watson.)

The 1984 Queen of Leon Valley is shown under the archway flanked by her two duchesses. They were attending the annual San Antonio Livestock Show and Rodeo as representatives from Leon Valley. Leon Valley is surrounded by the city of San Antonio and participates in many of its celebrations. (Courtesy of LVPL.)

On the occasion of Leon Valley's 40th anniversary, a time capsule was buried in front of city hall. Mayor Irene Baldridge (the last person with a shovel) stated in a newspaper article, "Leon Valley has very special people who are very interested in our community. We have hundreds of people involved with civic organizations and city commissions, and it's all volunteer." (Courtesy of LVPL.)

The Los Leones annual student art show was started about 15 years ago by Marcella "Marcy" Meffert and Lucy Garcia. The idea was not only to promote art among the students but to show that art is a business and one can make a living as an artist. Art students from the schools in the Northside Independent School District are invited to participate. In the beginning, about 400 students, teachers, and parents participated. It has since grown to over 3,600 participants. Both the community center and conference center, along with the green space, are utilized. Sidewalk art is also displayed. Food booths donate a percentage of their sales to the program. Prizes are awarded to elementary, middle, and high school winners of the contests. T-shirts are also available. Local businesses help sponsor the program. (Courtesy of LVPL.)

Shown here are Karen Peterson and her two daughters, Lauren (center) and Casey (right), watching the Leon Valley Parade in 1973. The Leon Valley Pageant Association sponsored an annual parade in which the Leon Valley Historical Society participated, usually with a float or a decorated vehicle. (Courtesy of K&EAHC.)

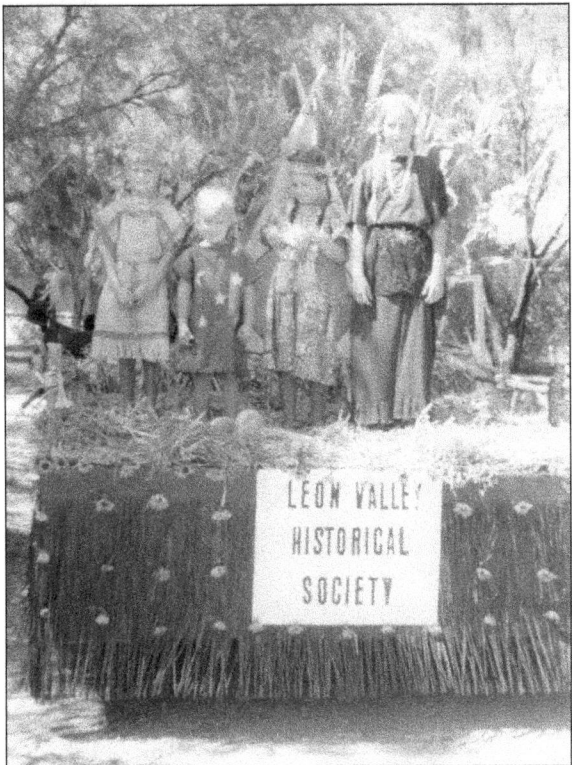

The Leon Valley Historical Society entry in the Leon Valley Stagecoach Days Parade was this pickup truck with the flatbed decorated with hay. The girls are dressed as Tonkawa Indian maidens. The Tonkawa Indians were once numerous in and around the Leon Valley area. (Courtesy of LVPL.)

Shown here is former mayor Marcella "Marcy" Meffert, second from right in the serving line, at the elegant Black Tie catered luncheon that was in honor of her book-signing party on October 21, 2006. The luncheon was sponsored by the Friends of the Leon Valley Public Library. Her book, entitled *Madam Mayor, How I Learned to Love Government and Hate Politics in Ten Intriguing Years*, was published earlier that year. After 20 years as wife, mother, and community volunteer, Marcy began a new career as a freelance and staff writer, columnist, and reporter for newspapers and magazines. She also worked as an editorial consultant on eight books for other authors. Beginning in 1994, she served four years as a councilmember and six years as mayor of Leon Valley. She was active on regional and state levels in various leadership roles. Her purpose in writing the book was to encourage more people to get seriously involved in government. (Courtesy of LVPL.)

The great lawn mower race was held on a bright fall day as a feature of the October 1983 Stagecoach Days celebration in Raymond Rimkus Park. No one remembers who won, but the park got mowed and a good time was had by all. (Courtesy of LVPL.)

The Star Spangled Leon Valley Kids carry their beribboned banner proudly down Poss Road accompanied by sponsors, bicycles, tricycles, wagons, happy parents, and an entourage of walkers in this early Fourth of July celebration. Leon Valley parades are an important part of "Leon Valley Pride." (Courtesy of K&EAHC.)

Shown in this photograph are, from left to right, (seated) Bea Miller, holding Shelly the mascot, and Jane Greer; (standing) Sophie Becerril, Peggy Bissett, Lin Robey, and Lois Murphy. Since 1978, the Friends of the Leon Valley Public Library has been a support organization for the Leon Valley Public Library. They have raised funds for projects, furnishings, computers, supplies, matching grants, and programs. In the past, they have been awarded the Annual Benefactors Award by the Texas Library Association and the Sweepstakes Award by the San Antonio Express News as the nonprofit of the year. More recently, they have been awarded two rural library initiative grants from the Kronkosky Charitable Foundation for collection enrichment, technology, facilities improvements, and special services enrichment. They have also participated in a collaborative grant from the Kronkosky Charitable Foundation for a Partnership for Parenting Education Project. A group of volunteers meet every Monday morning to price and shelve donated books, which are sold at book sales twice a year. (Courtesy of Carol Poss.)

Six

RECREATION AND PARKS

Leon Valley is a city rich in parks, recreational areas, and green space awaiting the young and young at heart. The library complex is known as the heart of the city. A community center, conference center, the Leon Valley Public Library, and the Huebner Creek enclose a large green lawn complete with a pavilion. The Huebner Creek forms the remaining north side of the quadrangle. Across Evers Road, a large stone monument marks the entrance to the 24-acre Raymond Rimkus Park, which has a number of picnic tables, a large pavilion with grills for roasting and barbecuing, a beautiful playground for youngsters of all ages, walking trails, a ball park, tennis courts, basketball courts, and soccer fields. Adjacent to the park, the 36-acre Huebner-Onion Natural Area, with its abundance of wildlife, trees, and native plants, invites walkers, hikers, and bird watchers to explore and enjoy nature. On Poss Road, close to the Huebner-Onion Natural Area, is the Northwest Little League Ball Park with snack bars and playing fields. Two swimming pools are available in the summer. A city-owned swimming pool is located in Grass Valley, and a neighborhood pool is located in Forest Oaks. Ongoing library programs for people of all ages are hosted throughout the year, and of course, there is always the annual Fourth of July Parade on Evers and Poss Roads.

Let's take a walk. Leaving the Raymond Rimkus Park and walking toward the Huebner-Onion Natural Area, grazing deer can sometimes be seen. They are often fed corn by the people in the homes nearby. A large wooden sign in the photograph below marks the entrance to the 36-acre natural area for hiking, jogging, bird watching, and wildlife observation. The sign indicates that it is open to the public from sunrise to sunset. It also asks that visitors pack in, pack out. No pets are allowed. The trails are primitive and wind around the area for a distance of about a mile and a half. (Courtesy of Carol Poss.)

This large wooden sign just past the entrance to the Huebner-Onion Natural Area indicates the trail to the 1882 Joseph Huebner gravesite. It is just a short walk through the wooded area to the gravesite. Prior to the purchase by the city, vandals had demolished the gravesite, scattering stones over a wide area. (Courtesy of LVHS.)

Pictured here is the condition of the Joseph Huebner gravesite before restoration. No death certificate was ever registered for Huebner, and the cause of death is not known. According to oral history, there may have been a child or infant also buried at the site. (Courtesy of LVHS.)

Working with the aid of the Leon Valley Public Works Department and an Eagle Scout and his troop, they restored the gravesite in 2002. Many of the stones were recovered, but more lime stones had to be brought in by the public works department. Leveling of the ground was the first step after the clearing of weeds, brush, and a few small trees. A cement mixer was brought in by the scouts. The city furnished a generator and gallons of water for the mixer. Measurements were taken, and it was determined that the limestone walls would measure 14 feet by 12 feet and be three feet high. The scouts and their volunteers worked a total of 639 hours on this project. Equipment and supplies furnished by the city cost $3,632. Upon completion, the gravesite was enclosed on all four sides by a three-foot wall of limestone rocks; a large square stone topped by an obelisk marked the center of the site. A six-foot chain link fence surrounds the site. (Courtesy of LVHS.)

Many of the large trees in the Huebner-Onion Natural Area have been here for hundreds of years, as shown in the photograph at right. Walking trails around the periphery of the Huebner-Onion Natural Area allow for firsthand observation of the over 35 species of plants that have been documented, including bluebonnets and cacti. Near the center of the property is the marshy area, shown in the photograph below, formed from a tributary of Huebner Creek, which runs from Seneca and Evers Roads through the middle of the Huebner-Onion Natural Area. In the catalog of wildlife, "catfish" is listed. This is where they live. Thirty-three species of birds, seven species of amphibians and reptiles, eight species of mammals, two types of butterflies, and five species of fish have been observed. (Both, courtesy of Carol Poss.)

Soccer teams come from all around the Leon Valley area to compete and practice at Raymond Rimkus Park. The majority of the teams come from the schools and organizations outside the city limits of Leon Valley. The 24-acre park provides a spacious area for youth and families. (Courtesy of LVPL.)

This mother and child go exploring along the Huebner Creek bed. After a good hard rain the creek flows for a few days. The creek floods after several days of really hard rain. When it does, Evers Road is often closed for a short time. (Courtesy of LVPL.)

This beautiful, handicapped-accessible playground was built by the City of Leon Valley in 1984 with assistance from the Rotary Club and a Bexar Community Development Block Grant. It was built on the site of a previous playground, which had been used by the children of Leon Valley for many years, and is designed for children ages 5 to 12. The sign recommends taking turns, no pushing or shoving, and using the equipment correctly. Adult supervision is required. The last recommendation is to, above all, have fun. This "Miracle Park" is located in the Raymond Rimkus Park on the corner of Poss and Evers Roads. (Both, courtesy of Carol Poss.)

Tennis courts are also available at the Raymond Rimkus Park. Here, a tennis coach instructs young students in the art and skill of tennis. On weekends, the courts are busy, particularly in the summertime. The park is open from sunrise to sunset. (Courtesy of LVPL.)

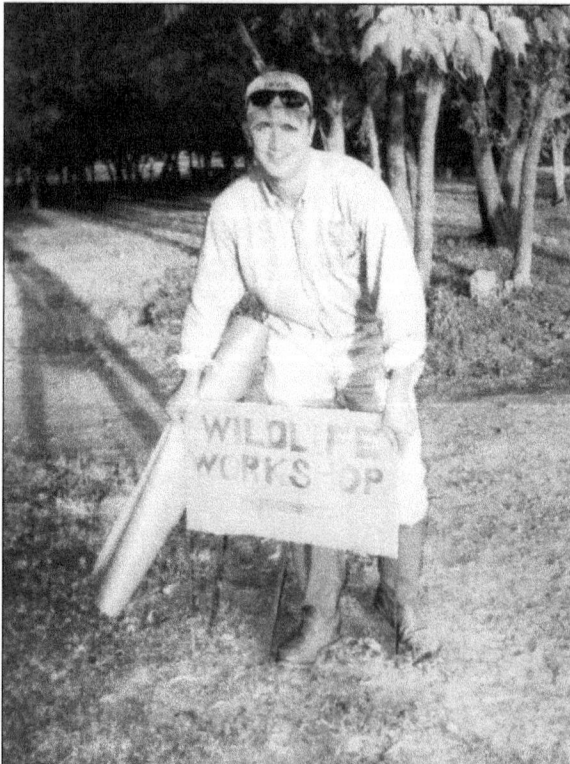

Standing by his sign in the Huebner-Onion Natural Area is Richard Heilbrun of the Texas Parks and Wildlife Department. The program took place around 2005 as part of the effort to educate local children about the many forms of wildlife in the Huebner-Onion Natural Area. (Courtesy of LVHS.)

This photograph, taken at the Raymond Rimkus Park at one of the Fourth of July celebrations, shows a potato-sack race in progress. The park covers more than 24 acres and is used by many residents and visitors to the city. (Courtesy of LVPL.)

A child from Leon Valley Elementary School proudly displays the animal tracks he has identified by making plaster casts of their paws. Children learned to identify different "critters" by their footprints and toured the area to learn about different species of plants and wildlife. (Courtesy of LVHS.)

The city of Leon Valley boasts two swimming pools for the summer enjoyment of its residents and their visitors. The city pool shown here is located in the Grass Valley subdivision at Strawflower and Larksong Drives and was built by the developer. It is across Poss Road from the Raymond Rimkus Park. A citizen committee managed it until about 2000, when it was necessary for the city to step in. The photograph below shows the Forest Oaks pool located at the corner of Evers Road and Forest Oaks Drive. It is currently managed by a committee of dedicated individuals in the area. (Both, courtesy of Carol Poss.)

Seven

MEMORABLE MOMENTS

From the beginning, especially with the efforts of the Leon Valley Pageant Association, citizens of Leon Valley have commemorated and celebrated their memorable moments. Each new event fosters a sense of community spirit. The city honors its heroes as the nation honors theirs by acknowledging their service in commemorative events. The Evers Cemetery lies within the city limits and has been commemorated with a dedication ceremony and Texas historical marker. City beautification and xeriscape programs are sponsored in coordination with master gardeners. Volunteers chauffeur the gardeners around the city to evaluate residential yards, business landscaping, and award signs that can be posted on site. Civic and community events involve students from local schools. This helps foster parent participation and adds to the spirit of each occasion. National Honor Society students from John Marshall High School have helped with the annual Breakfast with Santa program, and the Leon Valley Elementary School choir has sung at civic celebrations. The annual Los Leonas celebration invites students of all ages to display their art. Volunteers sponsor an annual Earthwise Living Day, which is an ecological, educational, and family event. Eagle Scout projects have been assisted by the Leon Valley Public Works Department. Leon Valley also enjoys two sister cities, one in Italy and the other in Australia. Some of the civic leaders have traveled to both these cities and also welcomed visitors in return.

The above photograph shows Maj. June Lee Neely Jr., right, in an F102 jet fighter cockpit with an unidentified trainee. Major Neely's disabled Air National Guard jet aircraft crashed near city hall on May 31, 1963. It appeared that he intentionally delayed his safe ejection in order to avoid the Leon Valley School and nearby heavily populated areas, thus allowing insufficient time for his parachute to open. No one on the ground was injured but Major Neely lost his life. The photograph at left shows a monument in front of city hall dedicated on October 27, 1990, to Major Neely's sacrifice, which was commemorated by the Historical Society of Leon Valley, the City of Leon Valley, and Texas Air National Guard. (Above, courtesy of J. Lee Neely III; left, courtesy of K&EAHC.)

Leon Valley resident L.Cpl. Stephen Joseph Perez, US Marine Corps, was killed in action in Anbar Province, Iraq, on April 13, 2006. He is the only Leon Valley serviceman to die, to date, in the Iraq/Afghanistan wars. Stephen made the ultimate sacrifice for his country. His heroic actions will never be forgotten by his friends and family. (Courtesy of LVPL.)

Retired Lt. Col. Dean Lewis Kennedy (who died at the age of 87 years in 2011) was a Leon Valley author and award-winning photographer. He was also a combat hero with 30 years service in the US Air Force. He served in Europe during World War II as a pilot, earning the Distinguished Flying Cross. Kennedy flew over 200 missions and earned two Bronze Stars during the Vietnam conflict. (Courtesy of LVPL.)

Richard "Sonny" Douglas McCullough, a young man born and raised in Leon Valley, enlisted in the navy in 1942. On July 17, 1943, at the age of 22 while on a training flight, he and the seven other men on board vanished in the Bermuda Triangle. The plane and crew were never found. (Courtesy of Gloria Anderson.)

At the dedication of the new Leon Valley Public Library, a banner honoring those who served in World War II was displayed. Karen Peterson points to the one Gold Star honoring her uncle, Richard McCullough, who was lost in World War II. Richard was a great-grandson of Heinrich Steubing Sr., an early settler in Leon Valley in the 1800s. (Courtesy of Gloria Anderson.)

The Evers Cemetery on Forest Pine Street in Leon Valley received its Texas State Historical Marker on May 16, 1992. The first burial in the cemetery was in the 1870s. A woman had stayed overnight at the Evers household because she had become ill traveling on the stagecoach from San Antonio. She died during the night and was buried under an oak tree. In the late 1870s, infant Annie Wehmeyer died and was buried close by. Not long after, Franz Wehmeyer, Annie's father, hit his knee with an axe, which resulted in amputation. The leg was buried in the cemetery. Shortly thereafter, Franz died and was buried near Annie. The cemetery is shown in the above photograph; the marker is seen at right. (Above, courtesy of Donna Maytum Christopher; right, courtesy of K&EAHC.)

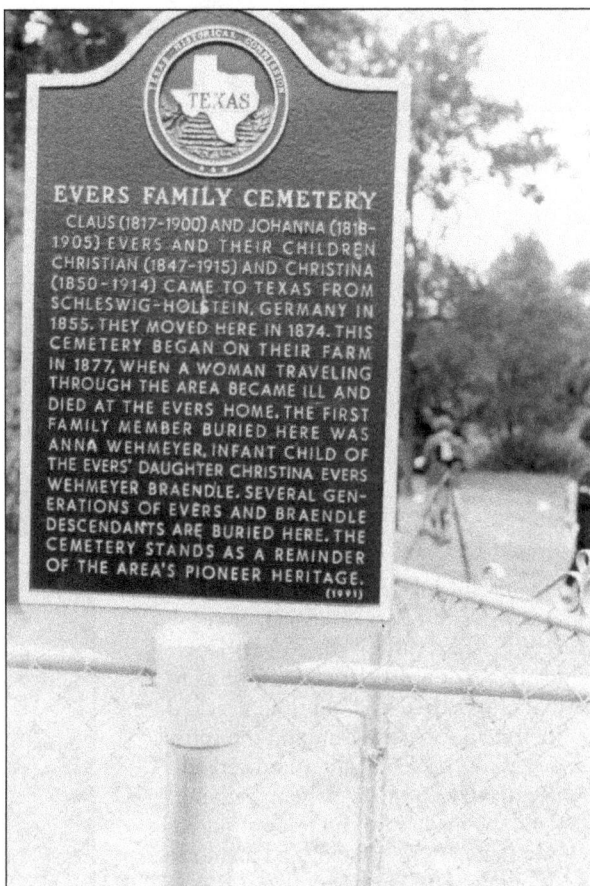

EVERS FAMILY CEMETERY

CLAUS (1817-1900) AND JOHANNA (1818-1905) EVERS AND THEIR CHILDREN CHRISTIAN (1847-1915) AND CHRISTINA (1850-1914) CAME TO TEXAS FROM SCHLESWIG-HOLSTEIN, GERMANY IN 1855. THEY MOVED HERE IN 1874. THIS CEMETERY BEGAN ON THEIR FARM IN 1877, WHEN A WOMAN TRAVELING THROUGH THE AREA BECAME ILL AND DIED AT THE EVERS HOME. THE FIRST FAMILY MEMBER BURIED HERE WAS ANNA WEHMEYER, INFANT CHILD OF THE EVERS' DAUGHTER CHRISTINA EVERS WEHMEYER BRAENDLE. SEVERAL GENERATIONS OF EVERS AND BRAENDLE DESCENDANTS ARE BURIED HERE. THE CEMETERY STANDS AS A REMINDER OF THE AREA'S PIONEER HERITAGE. (1991)

This photograph of two soldiers was taken in France on May 6, 1945. Edwin Menn is shown on the left. The Menn family owned a farm across the street from what is now John Marshall High School. Muriel Steubing (right) is the grandson of Henry Steubing Jr. (Courtesy of Dorothy Steubing Wright.)

This beautiful oak tree, still standing behind Arby's on Bandera Road, once graced the front yard of the Robert Doyle family home. It was behind a row of 25 to 30 mailboxes where the old-timers picked up their mail. Doyle was among the initial incorporators of Leon Valley and served on the first city council. When the land was sold, he made sure the tree would be maintained because it held fond memories of his children. (Courtesy of Carol Poss.)

Earthwise Living Day was founded in 1989 by Chris Riley, Rita Burnside, and Susan Butler. This educational, ecological, and family event features vendors, distributors, speakers, music, and performances by schoolchildren. A poetry contest sponsored by the Leon Valley Public Library began its first event with about eight tables for participants. It has become so popular that now 45 tables are needed. The event is held in the community center and the conference center. The above photograph show the sponsors, from left to right, Loretta Copponele, Darby Riley, Rita Burnside, Irene Baldridge, Lin Boudreau, Mary Key, and Chris Riley. The photograph at right shows the banner of Earthwise Living Day. (Both, courtesy of Rita Burnside.)

Frances Hillje, a longtime library patron, is honored on the occasion of her 100th birthday in October 2008 by her family, library staff, and volunteers. Library director Joyce Trent is shown holding the cake. A number of volunteers brought in their rocking chairs for this celebration. Hillje said she had "never felt so honored." (Courtesy of LVPL.)

Frances Hillje, with tiara and corsage, is surrounded by her smiling family. She remembers growing up in the age when the earliest automobiles were all the rage. In fact, she was born the very year that they were invented. She was also born the same year income tax was begun. (Courtesy of LVPL.)

Standing outside by the fire engines are several members of the Leon Valley Fire Department. Inside the department, a large, framed photograph is displayed on the wall. The photograph was taken in 1988 and shows the firemen who were involved in a dramatic rescue and a nine-week-old baby in the arms of fireman Fred Friar. When baby Jayme was five weeks old, her parents were traveling through Leon Valley on Bandera Road when Jayme stopped breathing. They stopped and tried to flag down someone. A woman stopped and suggested they take Jayme to the Leon Valley Fire Department, which was just a few blocks away. By the time they got there, Jayme was completely blue. The firemen worked on her, suctioned her, and gave her oxygen. She was taken to Methodist Hospital where she recovered with no permanent damage thanks to the quick and precise action of firemen Cosmo Alvizo, Mike Hacker, Paul Tejas, Vince Easley, Fred Friar, and Jeff Bailey. (Courtesy of K&EAHC.)

Philip Manwaring, a promising young athlete, was raised in the subdivision of Canterfield in Leon Valley. He played little league baseball with the Northwest Little League at Salazar Park. The classifications for little league baseball are Pee Wee, Minor, and Major divisions. At age 12, boys were required to enter the major league division of little league; however, Philip was promoted to the majors at an earlier age, about eight or nine, because he was such an excellent player. He also played Pop Warner football in middle school. During his freshman year at John Marshall High School, Philip played freshman football and basketball and was on the junior varsity baseball team. During that same year, in 1979, Philip succumbed to a brain tumor. The decision was made to name this little league baseball field in his honor. (Courtesy of Carol Poss.)

The two large bells outside city hall were installed about the year 2000. A civic-minded citizen, Lucy Garcia, urged Mayor Marcella "Marcy" Meffert (1998–2004) to consider having a bell to ring for special events, particularly at the end of elections after the votes were all in. Lucy found bells after searching diligently, and they were duly added in front of city hall. (Courtesy of Carol Poss.)

This picturesque well in front of the Leon Valley Conference Center was originally used by the Evers School and was located on the land now known as Monte Robles. When Huebner Road was being widened, the well was in danger of being demolished. Mayor Marcy Meffert had the well moved at her own expense to its present location. An Eagle Scout project restored the well with the help of the city's public works department. (Courtesy of Carol Poss.)

Taken from the side of the library porch, this photograph shows a memorable moment that most people would like to forget. When Huebner Creek overflowed its banks in 1998, floodwaters came within inches of the library porch. Inundating the Raymond Rimkus Park and the Huebner-Onion Natural Area and closing Bandera and Evers Roads, the floodwaters also entered city hall, the police department, and the fire station. Fire trucks were moved out of harm's way, and the homes on El Verde Road were evacuated. The Leon Valley Elementary School was the first shelter to open for evacuees. Horses were tethered to the school pillars. Water rose out of the banks of the Huebner Creek at the rear of the stagecoach stop to the base of the stack-stone barn but did not enter the barn, the cookhouse, or the homestead. Many changes, upgrades and improvements were made in the city as a consequence of this flood. (Courtesy of LVPL.)

Eight

SAVING A

STAGECOACH STOP

The Huebner-Onion Homestead and Stagecoach Stop at 6613 Bandera Road is one of the few homestead clusters of its era that is still standing. An Austrian immigrant, Joseph Huebner, established a stagecoach stop and homestead on this site in 1862. Many years later in 1930, Judge John F. Onion; his wife, Harriet; and their twin sons (they were age five) moved into the homestead, which was reportedly haunted. Members of this family have verified that creaking footsteps, sounds of glass breaking, and other weird sounds could not be explained. Folklore has it that Huebner liked to drink and occasionally drank too much. Once, when it could not be determined whether he was dead or dead drunk, he was buried. The haunting was attributed to Huebner. The Onion family made light of the situation because Harriet Onion did not want her sons to be afraid. In 2001, the Leon Valley Historical Society received the Huebner-Onion Homestead and Stagecoach Stop by gift from the adjacent Intown Suites. It intends to develop the homestead into a living history museum with a nature center in conjunction with the Huebner-Onion Natural Area. The society has raised funds to develop a master plan with the assistance of architects, museum designers, and other professionals. Continuing with their fundraising efforts, the society hopes to realize their goal in the not too distant future.

This is the Huebner-Onion Homestead as it appeared in 1984. Joseph Huebner built the lower floor of the house in 1862 and the upper floor in 1882. Later, he added the two-story porch with an upper balcony. After 1930, when the Onion family took up residence, a two-story east wing, a one-story kitchen, and a mudroom were added. Harriet Onion lived on the homestead after her husband's death in 1954 and remained there until shortly before her death in 1983 at the age of 93. The house was left with furnishings intact. Transients and vandals entered the house, as did raccoons, buzzards, and other wildlife. Several fires occurred over the years, and it suffered from the ravages of time and the weather. The house has survived Indian raids, fire, flooding, vandalism, and urbanization. (Courtesy of K&EAHC.)

This view of the exterior of the stagecoach stop shows the deterioration brought on by years of neglect and vandalism. Fires occurred within the home, charring the heavy overhead beams and destroying a portion of the roof. The masonry walls were in need of repair, and the porch wood was rotting. (Courtesy of LVHS.)

This view of the interior of the living room of the stagecoach stop shows the graffiti on the fireplace and walls left by vandals. Sunlight is entering through the partially destroyed roof, and an old bed spring is lying on the floor. Part of the fireplace has been removed. (Courtesy of Shirley Owen.)

The Huebner-Onion Homestead and Stagecoach Stop after "mothballing" is shown here in this 2002 photograph. The porch has been removed and the masonry repointed. The roof has also been replaced. The doors and windows are sealed to prevent unwelcome tenants, human or otherwise. The inscription etched in limestone at the rear door reads "1862." During the preservation, an old cypress post foundation measuring about 10 feet by 10 feet was found under the floor of the original part of the existing house. In order to give more interior space to the original great room, the inside staircase was moved outside and later enclosed with limestone walls. When Judge Onion remodeled the house in the 1930s, he made every effort to keep the original genre of the house intact. Keystones above the windows and doors of the additions after 1930 are diamond-topped compared to the original keystones, which are flat-topped. (Courtesy of Shirley Owen.)

The stack-stone barn of masonry and wooden construction is shown with the wood deteriorating and overgrown by weeds and trees. The barn is of unusual construction. Limestone rubble was used to level the stacked stones, and creek mud was used for mortar. This is one of only a few such barns left in Texas. (Courtesy of Shirley Owen.)

After replacement of rotted wood and repointing of masonry, the stack-stone barn is preserved for the future. Some heavy beams had been removed by trespassers before the barn was deeded to the historical society and needed to be replaced. Trees were trimmed back and shrubbery removed. (Courtesy of Shirley Owen.)

The third building in the homestead complex is called the cookhouse. It is a one-room, 11-foot-by-16-foot structure that was held together with creek mud as mortar and served as the original home for the Huebner family. The roof was gone and only two of the walls were intact. The limestone blocks were scattered around the area. The cornerstone is dated as 1858. (Courtesy of Shirley Owen.)

The cookhouse is shown after preservation. The stones in the two walls were replaced and the masonry of the walls repointed. Natural gas was not available and farm homes used wood for cooking. In hot summer weather, the house would stay cooler when cooking was done at a location away from the house. (Courtesy of Shirley Owen.)

This photograph, actually taken inside the Huebner-Onion Stagecoach Stop when it was occupied by the Onion family, shows Judge John F. "Pete" Onion and his wife, Harriet, seated in a recliner in the downstairs bedroom. A stuffed deer head can be seen in the upper right corner. The date is probably sometime in the late 1950s. (Courtesy of Frank Onion.)

Linda Persyn, president of the Leon Valley Historical Society, presides over the deed announcement on March 22, 2001, which was the time the Huebner-Onion Homestead and Stagecoach Stop and 0.567 acres was sold to the Leon Valley Historical Society by Intown Suites. The celebration was held on the grounds of the stagecoach stop. (Courtesy K&EAHC.)

The annual fundraising dinners to raise money for the restoration were called the "Bloomin' Onion Dinners" and were held in the community center with Outback Steakhouse serving the meal. Shown on stage are Hank Harrison and his Bluegrass Band, who played for these events. Silent auctions and a raffle added to the festivities. (Courtesy of LVHS.)

At the Bloomin' Onion Dinner in 2006, among the many guests who attended was Frank Onion, grandson of Judge John F. Onion. He is shown here in an animated conversation with three of the great-granddaughters of stagecoach stop proprietor Joseph Huebner. (Courtesy of LVHS.)

116

Docia Schultz Williams is shown boarding the chartered bus for a tour of haunted houses in San Antonio. The Leon Valley Historical Society sponsored the tour. Williams and coauthor Reneta Byrne were authors of the book *Spirits of San Antonio and South Texas*, published in 1993. The cover of the book shows an artist's rendition of the stagecoach stop and the ghost proprietor Joseph Huebner. (Courtesy of Linda Persyn.)

These smiling boys, with their parents in the background, were part of a Cub Scout tour of the Huebner-Onion Stagecoach Stop and Natural Area conducted by Leon Valley Historical Society members. This photograph, taken in 2010, also shows the Huebner Creek bed, which runs behind the homestead and winds along the Huebner-Onion Natural Area. (Courtesy of Darby Riley.)

The sorghum/molasses press was moved to the Huebner-Onion Homestead behind the cookhouse by Bob McWilliams, from the Texas Amateur Archeological Association, and Thomas Fryer. Standing next to the press are, from left to right, Bob McWilliams, Thomas Fryer, Gloria Anderson (who raised money for the plaque), and Evelyn Shaw. In the foreground is the painting by Emilio Torres, illustrating how the press worked. (Courtesy of Barbara Fryer.)

The sorghum/molasses cane press is installed in back of the cookhouse at the homestead. The inscription reads, "Sorghum Cane Press/Juice was boiled to make molasses syrup / Donated by Mr. and Mrs. O.F. 'Bob' Burns from their farm in Leon Valley / Formerly owned by Mr. and Mrs. Henry Steubing who installed and used the press from 1890 to 1945." (Courtesy of Barbara Fryer.)

118

Shirley Owen, Leon Valley Historical Society archivist, and Sue Ann Pemberton, owner of Mainstreet Architects, stand by the plaque on the homestead on May 12, 2008. The Leon Valley Historical Society and the San Antonio Conservation Society celebrated the dedication of the Huebner-Onion Homestead and Stagecoach Stop as part of the National Register of Historic Places and as a Texas Historical Landmark. (Courtesy of Barbara Fryer.)

With Frank Onion at the microphone, the Leon Valley Historical Society celebrated its second Pioneer Ice Cream Social in 2010. Shown in front of the homestead are, from left to right, Joey Tomlinson, the master of ceremonies; Frank Onion; Sidney Yarbrough, from the San Antonio Conservation Society; and Darby Riley, president of Leon Valley Historical Society. (Courtesy of LVHS.)

Mel Ellenwood, chuck wagon cooker at the Pioneer Ice Cream Social in 2010, tries to impress the mannequin from the Northside School District Museum but finds her unresponsive. Not even the delicious peach cobbler from the chuck wagon made any impression. (Courtesy of Barbara Fryer.)

Mike Walsh, farrier, stands by his anvil with tools in hand at the Pioneer Ice Cream Social in 2008, ready to demonstrate his craft. Among the other participants were a cowboy trick roper, a chuck wagon cooker, quilters, and the Alamo Lore and Myth Organization with antique firearms. (Courtesy of LVHS.)

These two boys from Intown Suites are holding mule shoes found in the Huebner Creek bed during the 2010 Pioneer Ice Cream Social. The blacksmith identified the artifacts as mule shoes because they curve out at the tips instead of going straight up as horseshoes do. (Courtesy of LVHS.)

The El Camino Real International Pony Express Ride 2001 Heritage event began in front of the Leon Valley Huebner-Onion Stagecoach Stop on its way to Bandera, Texas, on April 14, 2001. Pictured among the riders are two members of the Leon Valley Historical Society in period costumes. (Courtesy of LVPL.)

This color guard Scout group participated in the Pioneer Ice Cream Social in 2010 at the Huebner-Onion Stagecoach Stop celebration. Bandera Road is shown in the background. Many civic organizations in the surrounding Leon Valley area are interested in seeing the old homestead restored. (Courtesy of LVHS.)

Hank Harrison and the Tennessee Valley Authority entertain at the Pioneer Ice Cream Social in 2010. This band has generously given of their time and talents at fundraising dinners and other events ever since the effort to preserve and restore the homestead began. Shown from left to right are Hank Harrison (fiddle/mandolin), Mary Ann Cornelius (acoustic bass), Mark Maniscalco (guitar), and Don Van Winkle (banjo). (Courtesy of LVHS.)

Four members of the San Antonio Conservation Society stand ready to dispense free ice cream at the 2010 Pioneer Ice Cream Social. The conservation society has been very supportive with grant funding and involvement with the preservation and restoration of the stagecoach stop. (Courtesy of LVHS.)

Shown here are two officers of the Northside Independent School District Museum at their cookbook sales booth and display during the 2010 Pioneer Ice Cream Social. Dorothy Warras, president, is on the right and Clementine Rodriguez, secretary, is holding the cookbook. (Courtesy of LVHS.)

Pictured here are several of the 50 homing pigeons that were released at the 2008 Pioneer Ice Cream Social. Kenneth and Beverly Pair of the Lazy P. Woodlawn Club Racing Pigeons released the pigeons in honor of the organization's namesake families and supporters, donors, partners, grantors, stakeholders, restoration specialists, architects, and Leon Valley Historical Society members. (Courtesy of LVHS.)

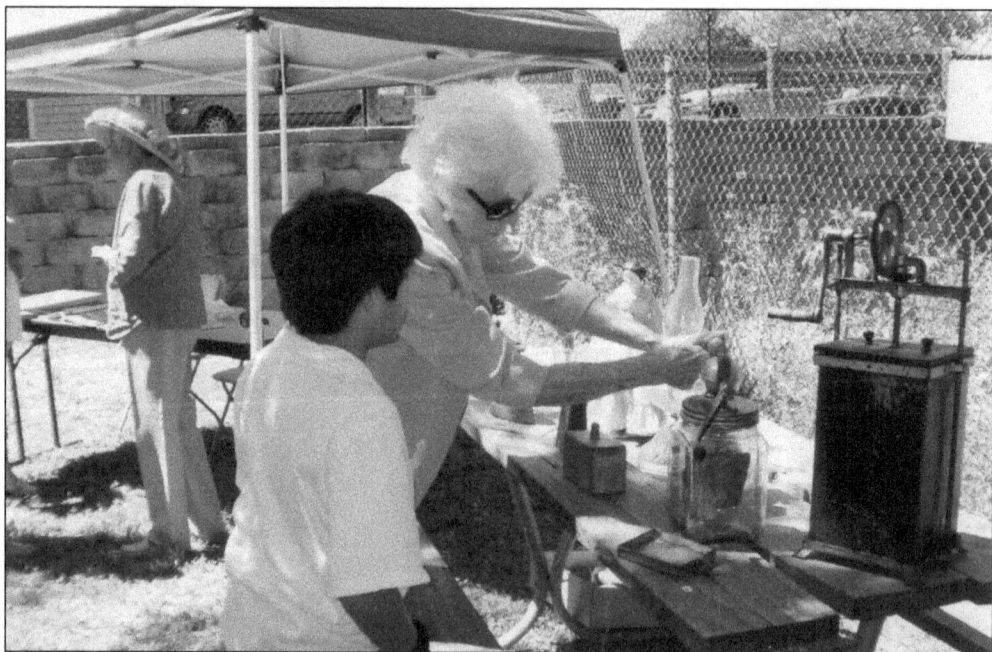

Evelyn Shaw, Leon Valley Historical Society member, shows a young guest at the 2010 Pioneer Ice Cream Social how the old butter churn works. Many early tools and implements from the pioneer days, including cowboy spurs, a corn stripper, animal traps, and a branding iron, were on display. (Courtesy of LVHS.)

Prof. Felix Almarez from the University of Texas at San Antonio stands by the Huebner-Onion Texas Historical Landmark as it is being unveiled at the Pioneer Ice Cream Social on May 18, 2008. Professor Almarez has been a supporter of the restoration of the stagecoach stop since the beginning of the project. (Courtesy of Sherry Watson.)

When Carl's Jr. opened their new restaurant on Bandera and Eckhert Roads in 2009, they shared with the Leon Valley Historical Society their desire to carry on the spirit of community involvement and family values of their founder Carl Karcher. They donated $500 toward saving the stagecoach stop and also contributed to other organizations. Pictured here are Carl's Jr. executives, Leon Valley Historical Society board members, and representatives of other recipients. (Courtesy of Carl's Jr. Restaurant.)

The officers of the Friends of Leon Valley Public Library are, from left to right (seated) treasurer Barbara Fryer, secretary Shirley Loban, and vice president Beatrice Miller; (standing) president Carol Poss and library director Joyce Trent. Incorporated in 1978 as a nonprofit organization, the Friends of Leon Valley Public Library promote the interest and welfare of the Leon Valley Public Library as a cultural and educational asset to the city of Leon Valley and the surrounding area. Combining the interests of both residents and businesses, the nonprofit has ensured that the library will have the extra resources that it needs to continue to be the "heart of the city." (Courtesy of LVPL.)

The officers and board of directors of the Leon Valley Historical Society are, from left to right, consultant Ed Conroy, treasurer Barbara Fryer, corresponding secretary Mark Eisenhauer, recording secretary Pam Weatherford, vice president Irene Baldridge, president Darby Riley, advisor Dr. Robert Dons, memorial trust officer Carol Poss, and past president Linda Persyn. Archivist Shirley Owen is not pictured. Incorporated in 1973 as part of the Leon Valley Pageant Association, the nonprofit organization has, for over 30 years, continually promoted, celebrated, and compiled the history of Leon Valley and the surrounding area. It is also dedicated to the restoration and operation of the Huebner-Onion Homestead and Stagecoach Stop as a living history museum and nature center in conjunction with the 36-acre natural area. (Courtesy of LVHS.)

Visit us at
arcadiapublishing.com